T0362913

PUBLISHED BY BOOM BOOKS

boombooks.biz

ABOUT THIS SERIES

....But after that, I realised that I knew very little about these parents of mine. They had been born about the start of the Twentieth Century, and they died in 1970 and 1980. For their last 20 years, I was old enough to speak with a bit of sense.

I could have talked to them a lot about their lives. I could have found out about the times they lived in. But I did not. I know almost nothing about them really. Their courtship? Working in the pits? The Lock-out in the Depression? Losing their second child? Being dusted as a miner? The shootings at Rothbury? My uncles killed in the War? Love on the dole? There were hundreds, thousands of questions that I would now like to ask them. But, alas, I can't. It's too late.

Thus, prompted by my guilt, I resolved to write these books. They describe happenings that affected people, real people. The whole series is, to coin a modern phrase, designed to push your buttons, to make you remember and wonder at things forgotten.

The books might just let nostalgia see the light of day, so that oldies and youngies will talk about the past and re-discover a heritage otherwise forgotten. Hopefully, they will spark discussions between generations, and foster the asking and answering of questions that should not remain unanswered.

BORN IN 1968?

WHAT ELSE HAPPENED?

RON WILLIAMS

AUSTRALIAN SOCIAL HISTORY

BOOK 30 IN A SERIES OF 32
FROM 1939 to 1970

War Babies Years (1939 to 1945):   7 Titles
Baby Boom Years (1946 to 1960):   15 Titles
Post Boom Years (1961 to 1968):   10 Titles

BOOM, BOOM BABY, BOOM

PUBLISHED BY BOOM BOOKS

Wickham, NSW, Australia

Web: www.boombooks.biz

Email: email@boombooks.biz

© Ron Williams 2013. This edition 2019

A single chapter or part thereof may be copied and reproduced without permission, provided that the Author, Title, ISBN and Web Site are acknowledged.

Creator: Williams, Ron, 1934- author.

Title: Born in 1968? : what else happened? / Ron Williams.

Edition: Premier edition

ISBN: 9780995354913

Australia--History--Miscellanea--20th century.

Cover image: National Archives of Australia   A1200, L3639, PM John Gorton; A1200, L54943, Aboriginal typist/telephonist at work; A1200, L48577, Family washing car; A1200, L53790, Family breakfast; A1200, L55381, Men at work on oil drilling rig.

TABLE OF CONTENTS

IMPORTANT PEOPLE AND EVENTS

Queen of England	Elizabeth II
Prime Minister of Oz	John Gorton
Leader of Opposition	Gough Whitlam
Governor General	Lord Richard Casey
The Pope	Paul VI
US President	Lyndon Johnson
PM of Britain	Harold Wilson

Winner of the Ashes:

1965 - 6	Drawn	1 - 1
1968	Drawn	1 - 1
1970 - 71	England	2 - 0

Melbourne Cup Winners:

1967	Red Handed
1968	Rain Lover
1969	Rain Lover

Academy Awards, 1968:

Best Actor	Rod Steiger
Best Actress	Katharine Hepburn

PREFACE TO THIS SERIES

This book is the 30th in a series of books that I have researched and written. It tells a story about a number of important or newsworthy Australia-centric events that happened in 1968. The series covers each of the years from 1939 to 1968, for a total of 30 books.

I developed my interest in writing these books a few years ago at a time when my children entered their teens. My own teens started in 1947, and I tried to remember what had happened to me then. I thought of the big events first, like Saturday afternoon at the pictures, and cricket in the back yard, and the wonderful fun of going to Maitland on the train for school each day. Then I recalled some of the not-so-good things. I was an altar boy, and that meant three or four Masses a week. I might have thought I loved God at that stage, but I really hated his Masses. And the schoolboy bullies, like Greg Favel and the hapless Freddie Bevin. Yet, to compensate for these, there was always the beautiful, black headed, blue-sailor-suited June Brown, who I was allowed to worship from a distance.

I also thought about my parents. Most of the major events that I lived through came to mind readily. But after that, I realised that I really knew very little about these parents of mine. They had been born about the start of the Twentieth Century, and they died in 1970 and 1980. For their last 20 years, I was old enough to speak with a bit of sense. I could have talked to them a lot about their lives. I could have found out about the times they lived in. But I did not. I know almost nothing about them really. Their courtship? Working in the pits? The Lock-out in the Depression?

Losing their second child? Being dusted as a miner? The shootings at Rothbury? My uncles killed in the War? There were hundreds, thousands of questions that I would now like to ask them. But, alas, I can't. It's too late.

Thus, prompted by my guilt, I resolved to write these books. They describe happenings that affected people, real people. In 1968, there is some coverage of international affairs, but a lot more on social events within Australia. This book, and the whole series is, to coin a modern phrase, designed to push the reader's buttons, to make you remember and wonder at things forgotten. The books might just let nostalgia see the light of day, so that oldies and youngies will talk about the past and re-discover a heritage otherwise forgotten. Hopefully, they will spark discussions between generations, and foster the asking and the answering of questions that should not remain unanswered.

The sources of my material. I was born in 1934, so that I can remember well a great deal of what went on around me from 1939 onwards. But of course, the bulk of this book's material came from research. That meant that I spent many hours in front of a computer reading electronic versions of newspapers, magazines, Hansard, Ministers' Press releases and the like. My task was to sift out, day-by-day, those stories and events that would be of interest to the most readers. Then I supplemented these with materials from books, broadcasts, memoirs, biographies, government reports and statistics. And I talked to old-timers, one-on-one, and in organised groups, and to Baby Boomers about their recollections. People with stories to tell came out of the woodwork, and talked no end about the tragic, and funny, and commonplace events that have shaped their lives.

The presentation of each book. For each year covered, the end result is a collection of short Chapters on many of the topics that concerned ordinary people in that year.

I think I have covered most of the major issues that people then were interested in. On the other hand, in some cases I have dwelt a little on minor frivolous matters, perhaps to the detriment of more sober considerations. Still, in the long run, this makes the book more readable, and hopefully it will convey adequately the spirit of the times.

Each of the books is mainly Sydney based, but I have been **deliberately national in outlook**, so that readers elsewhere will feel comfortable that I am talking about matters that affected them personally. After all, housing shortages and strikes and juvenile delinquency involved **all** Australians, and other issues, such as problems overseas, had no State component in them. Overall, I expect I can make you wonder, remember, rage and giggle equally, no matter whence you hail.

INTRODUCTION TO 1968

The post-war world. By the time that the Japanese precipitated WWII in the Pacific by bombing Pearl Harbour, the major European powers had been scavenging the world looking for colonies for over two centuries.

As a result, Britain, France, Holland, Portugal, Spain, and Germany by 1940 had Empires and footholds that spread across the continents and oceans of the world. Some of them were called Dominions, like Australia and New

Zealand and Canada, and these had self-government. Others, generally smaller, were called colonies, and these included countries like Vietnam, Cambodia and Laos, and also kingdoms, as well as simple islander villages living on Pacific islands.

But whatever and wherever they existed, the flags of the European masters dominated their skylines, and they lived under the law of the colonial power who had got there first.

All of this was not always bad. The colonists brought with them education and better health and employment and law and order. They created local industries, and international trade. They built grand structures and held even grander spectacles. They were, from their own point of view, truly benefactors.

But the apparent bonhomie was interrupted by WWII. This world-wide catastrophe released every one of these dependencies from the constraints put on them pre-war. The Great Powers would have collapsed without the military help from their Empires, and now **those** Empires wanted their reward. So, by the end of the war, almost every dominion or colony who did not have self-government, wanted it badly.

For the next 20 or 30 years, and sometimes beyond, nationalist movements sought to get rid of the colonial powers from their soil. Every one of them had their own way of doing this, but one popular way was to take up the arms they had learned to use in the war, and form rebellious armies that were prepared to fight the colonialists for their lands and seas.

WAR IN VIETNAM.

Vietnam, still more or less under French control, was divided into two separate States, North and South Vietnam. The North had a common border with Communist China, and thus strong economic and military ties with that country. During the 1950's, the North and South came to blows in a serious way, and this carried over into the sixties. But now the USA slowly entered and transformed the small-scale internal war into a major international conflict.

The US thought that the Communists, represented by the North and China, were about to expand southwards through the South, and continue down until they had conquered Tasmania. **The Chinese** were intent on expanding the sphere of influence of Communism throughout all of South East Asia, starting with nearby Vietnam. Thus, by 1968, China and the US were locked in a bitter and ever-escalating ideological war, being fought on someone else's territory, in the North and South of Vietnam.

Australia, since the War, had gradually come to rely on America for its defence against aggression. So, in the mid-sixties, when the US decided to build up its armed forces in Vietnam, we responded by sending our advisers to that same location. Inevitably, this number of advisers increased, and their roles were expanded, so that by 1968 we had thousands of soldiers, Air Force and Navy fighting there,

This caused two immediate problems. The first was that a **dozen Australian Servicemen were being killed in action every month.** That was enough to unsettle all Australians.

The second was that over half of these men were **conscripted 20-year-olds** who had been plucked randomly from their families, put into uniforms, and sent off to the war zone. **All the current resistance to the war stemmed from this.**

Let me make **the case for the opposition to the war**. Families with male youngsters could see **that their sons** could be forced into the Army, sent off to a war zone, and **killed** there. The families, and don't forget the sons themselves, did not know about, or care one hoot about, this place Vietnam, or the supposed badness of the Reds, or their vile plans to recruit the world. **Few of them could see why we were in this war at all**, and their families and friends and others were prepared to fight any way they legally could to bring the boys back home.

At the start of 1968, protests were the order of the day, demonstrations were held in cities and towns by the hundreds, politicians and supporters of the war were abused and threatened, and mothers and fathers waited at home dreading the telegram from the Army that said their son was dead.

This was a terrible time for the nation. **Supporters** of the war genuinely thought and felt that the war was protecting us from a terrible fate. **Opponents** were sure that the war was useless, and simply a way to stay in good with our Yankee friends. There was no half-way point, no compromise. You were either **for or against** the war. And if you were on the other side of this issue, you were fair game for vocal abuse and contempt.

This brings us up to date. Over the coming pages, I will take up the Vietnam story. I will not dwell on the well-known military aspects of this, but will instead direct my efforts to **talking about the social consequences of the war** as it quickly developed and caused more and more divisions across this previously sleepy and contented nation.

KIDS STUFF

The days of the Baby Boom were over, but " the products of the womb" or, if you like "the products of the loins" during the post-war years, were making themselves visible. **Baby Boomers were everywhere. Or so it seemed.** Some of these were born in the late Forties, and were now aged about 20 and getting ready to start their own Echo to the Baby Boom. Others were teenagers, and some scrubbers had not yet reached that elite age. As one Letter-writer put it, "they are all over the bloody place."

They had the numbers, more than ever before. Their parents thought they were wonderful and talked about them all the time, the Press and advertisers exploited their every move. So, **they too** thought they were wonderful. Not just that, they were secure in the knowledge that they were the smartest, richest, mobile-est, prettiest, and coolest youths in history.

Be that as it may, they were obviously here to stay, and I will use the rest of this Introduction to talk more about them, and at the same time fill you in a little about the background to 1968.

At the moment, the Press was full of them organising into gangs who bashed and robbed taxi drivers, and drunks in parks. They were particularly fond of locating poofters who frequented public toilets at night and then belting the living daylights out of them.

They had souped up cars with all the noise that you might expect, and with a highly undesirable safety record. Young girls were sometimes promiscuous, and it appears some were wasting police time by often running away from home.

Even the Boy Scouts and Girl Guides were becoming pains in the neck. Granted scouting was very popular, but sometimes they annoyed the older generations. **Letters** appeared complaining about scouts destroying the Sunday afternoon nap with their Bob-a-Job requests. Guides were equally offensive with the selling of cakes and cosmetics.

These groups were also pushing Councils for more parklands to be given up to them so that they could build Scout Halls on them. These Halls were seen by some to be alienating public land for spoiled youngsters, a source of noise day and night, and a parking and traffic menace. And, so Letters said, they attracted "bums and hobos" who broke in and slept nights there.

But the worst of all were the teeny-boppers who, before school, hit themselves with half a dozen powders and pills. Then they sat in class in a drug induced twilight zone, their minds dazed and senses dulled.

Comment. Drugs, as we know them today, were just now in their infancy.

Generally, too, **they were seen as not conforming to the religions.** The fear of God and the fear of eternal damnation for sins committed was being replaced by belief that God would be more impressed by **positive** applications of religious deeds. And on top of that, there was an increasing and slowly-growing number of Christians who rejected their faith completely. Press articles about their "rejection of religion" were prominent and common.

Summing up. In fact, though, these supposed miscreants were no better or worse then their parents or other oldies. The Press, as usual, saw a way to exploit their every action and laid it on thick. The main differences were that they had more freedom than their parents, and more money, and more mobility. And, of course, they had more permissive parents who themselves were realising that the pre-War doldrums and conservatism served no useful purpose.

THE BABY BONUS

Can you believe it? Despite the hordes of little blighters running amok as mentioned above, the Government implemented a Baby Bonus plan. This would give a sum of money to any one who could bring a new-born ankle-biter into the world. The idea was to pay for the medical costs involved.

This was part of the Federal Government's policy of *Populate or Perish*. It thought that we had such a small population that we could not defend ourselves against attack from overseas, and so we needed to have more babies as quickly as possible,

Comment. No one can say from the statistics whether this scheme actually worked. But it did coincide with the natural Echo Baby Boom and with massive migration so, scheme or no scheme, the population started to boom again.

MY RULES IN WRITING

Now we are just about ready to go. First, though, I give you a few Rules I follow as I write. They will help you understand where I am coming from.

Note. Throughout this book, I rely a lot on reproducing **Letters from the newspapers**. Whenever I do this, I put the text in a different font, and indent it a little, and make the font somewhat smaller. **I do not edit the text at all. The same is true for the *News Items* at the start of each Chapter.** That is, I do not correct spelling or grammar, and if the text gets at all garbled, I do not correct it. It's just as it was seen in the Papers.

Second Note. The **material** for this book, when it comes from newspapers, is reported as it was seen at the time. If the benefit of hindsight over the years changes things, then I might record that in my Comments. **The info reported thus reflects matters as they were seen in 1968.**

Third Note. Let me also apologise in advance to anyone I might offend. In a work such as this, it is certain some people will think **I got some things wrong. I am sure that I did**, but please remember, all of this is only my opinion. And really, **my opinion does not matter one little bit in the scheme of things**. I hope you will say "silly old bugger", and shrug your shoulders, and read on.

OFF WE GO

So now we are ready to plunge into 1968. Let's go, and I trust you will have a pleasant trip.

JANUARY NEWS ITEMS

On December 17th last, at Portsea on the edge of Melbourne, **the Prime Minister Harold Holt was drowned.** He had been swimming **alone** in a high surf, on a deserted beach, and he simply disappeared. An intensive search failed to find his body, which has been missing ever since....

The Deputy Prime Minister, John McEwen, was sworn in as PM a few days later in an Acting role....

The new PM would be chosen by a vote among elected Liberals on January 9.

Comment. Observers all round the world **were amazed** that a person in a high position, such as a Prime Minister, **could go for a swim without adequate security.** On the other hand, all Australians rejoiced at the thought that **we had here a society that was hardly conscious of the threats** of all sorts that other national leaders were subject to.

The first edition of the Sydney Morning Herald (*SMH*) for the year was happy to announce that a couple in the NSW country town of Tenterfield were **now the proud parents of quintuplets. They already have a pair of twins, under the age of one**, as well as two other children. It seems at the moment that **the quins are doing well, after a hectic birth period of 75 minutes**.

A few years ago, in racially-divided **South Africa, Dr Christian Barnard had performed the world's first heart transplant.** This was at a time when **blood** transfusions between blacks and whites could only be done with the recipient's permission....

Now a **dying black girl was prepared to give her heart to a white man**. **Controversy erupted**, but the Barnard team went ahead. **The heart was not rejected** as many thought it would be, and the operation was successful....

Comment. In Australia, the White Australia Policy was under siege at the moment. One argument against relaxing the ban on Asians immigrating here was the claim that if an Asian gave blood to an Australian, **it would dilute our stock of pure British blood in our collective bodies, and thereby reduce our racial superiority.**

The Brits are facing up to economic realities. Harold Wilson, **the Prime Minister** announced that **its military forces "east of Suez" would be cut drastically from now**. That includes the support for the historic Indian Gurkhas, and for regions round the Persian Gulf....

For Australia, this meant that we were **now officially on our own in defence matters**. Since WWII when Britain offered us very little support, there had been **various pretenses** that Britain could and would support us if attacked. But now that these promises were no longer, **our reliance on the USA became more obvious**, and **we quickly got further into bed with the US**....

As one newspaper bitterly reported, the Brits cut their **military support for Australia** at the same time as **they stopped providing free milk to their own primary school students.**

PICKING A PM

The sudden death of Harold Holt threw the Liberals into confusion. Obviously they needed a leader who would also become Prime Minister. But they needed to be quick about it, because they had less than a month to make that decision. The problem for them was that Christmas was just around the corner, and that was followed by the New Year. Of course that meant that **the nation shut down for this period, and that normally included the politicians**. When they came back from the break, they had only a week to scramble round and plot and connive. But they faced up bravely to the task, and kept the media fully informed of their every frantic move.

Who would become Prime Minister? The naive first thought was **"Black" Jack McEwen**. After all, he was **Deputy** Prime Minister, and he was doing a good job as Minister for Trade. But there were forces against him. **Firstly**, he had said that if Billy McMahon (see later) was elected to leadership, then he would **not** remain as Deputy. And he went on to talk in vague terms about McMahon's unsuitability for the high position. **He made the startling statement that he did not trust McMahon.**

In the critical pre-poll limelight, **this Party split** got a hostile reception in many quarters.

> **Letters, W Dun.** What is Mr McEwen being so secretive about? Does he consciously know the damage he can cause by vague smears? Surely, since he started this controversy, he can now speak plainly in fairness to an opponent and be prepared to debate his case publicly with Mr McMahon.

He had his supporters though.

Letters, C Muir. I consider Mr McEwen should be persuaded to **continue as Prime Minister for at least three to five years** while a man of similar character and integrity is gaining experience and proving his ability to undertake such a "job" and not be just a mouthpiece of bureaucrats or one whose chief interest is "self."

Beyond that, he was not a Liberal. Rather, he came from the Country Party. Granted these two Parties were in a Coalition that, between themselves, gave them the numbers to hold power. But the Liberals, by far, held the reins, and it was generally thought that a Country Party representative would never get the nod from his Liberal colleagues.

Then there was a number of Liberals who had their eyes on the post. **A favourite was Bill McMahon.** He had been round for a long time, he had a lot of experience as a Minister, and he had a good looking wife who gave the Press a lot to talk about.

The Press was full of Letters that gave him support.

Letters, (Senator) J Ormonde. The rank and file of the Liberal Party will be pretty ungrateful to Mr McMahon if they don't give him a vote in the ballot to elect a leader. Only for Mr McMahon, many of them might never have been in Parliament.

Was it not in the fertile and ingenious brain of the Commonwealth Treasurer that the State aid "science block" legislation was hatched, and what an election gimmick that was! I'll never forget the evening in Parliament the Prime Minister made the sensational announcement. Government Members nearly fell from their seats, Mr McMahon had a smile from ear to ear. He knew.

Then again was it not Mr McMahon as Commonwealth Treasurer who sold Mr Johnson, the American

President, the idea of extending his Philippine tour to doing a **bit of baby kissing for Mr Holt**. And of course the Holt version of the American alliance was born with such happy results for the Government.

Yes, the Liberals have much to thank Mr McMahon for.

Letters, K McCarthy. Several of those now trying to win the position of Prime Minister have failed in various ministerial positions and have not been loyal to their then leaders. This cannot be said of Billy McMahon who has proved himself outstanding in the capacity of Treasurer of Australia. Billy may not be the most popular Minister in the race, but he has done each ministerial job given him efficiently and has always been loyal to his leader. How can his rivals, who have been failures as Ministers, demand to be Prime Minister because they have winning ways but no real ability.

Letters, E Trembath. Mr McMahon has made an outstanding success of every duty to which he has been delegated. At no time has he attempted to convey a personal image, but at all times his energies have been devoted to serving his country.

Mind you, it was not all one way. McMahon had his detractors.

Letters, W Hill. I have always been a Liberal with the welfare of my country very much at heart, and I want the very best man available, irrespective of party, for my Prime Minister.

When one remembers the tactics employed by Mr McMahon in the recent Capricornia by-election, it is incredible that a person who would stoop to this level should even be mentioned in connection with this high office. To my mind, a Prime Minister should be a man who inspires respect and confidence because of his character, vision and qualities of leadership - in short, a man one can look up to.

Still, when he went into the meeting of the combined Coalition Parties, McMahon would have thought himself favourite.

But the dark horse was the quiet, supposedly "sophisticated" challenger with a glamorous war record. This was **Senator John Gorton** who had recently held the position of Minister for Education and Science, and had done pretty well. In the last week he had been mentioned a few times in the Press, but mostly as a possible **Deputy** PM. Of the 30 Letters that I recently reviewed for this article, he was mentioned only three times. Two of these were unfavourable.

For example, "John Gorton was responsible for the severe restrictions on University grants, which led to the curtailment of so much research."

A third one, however, spoke well of him.

There were other Letters that offered **suggestions**. Quite a few said that the assembled Parliamentarians should follow their conscience, and not vote for a person from their home State.

Letters, R Healey. Once again, this time on the question of a choice of successor to the late Mr Holt, by the Liberal Party, it appears that the world will receive yet another demonstration of the lack of unity and jealousy between the six States comprising the Commonwealth.

If the Liberal Party really desires to raise a suitable memorial to its late lamented leader and Federal Prime Minister it should endeavour to choose a successor who is **an Australian first** and a Victorian, New South Welshman or Queenslander, etc., last of all.

One writer said their names should be drawn from a barrel, at random, the same way as our young Servicemen were selected for Vietnam.

Letters, J Burke. In order to facilitate the election of a new Prime Minister, the Coalition Government should be consistent and resort to its established practice of putting the names of all aspirants into a barrel (this is done in regard to conscripts for Vietnam), the first name drawn to be our new Prime Minister.

Thus, the question of personalities intruding would be disposed of. The successful contender would become the interim Prime Minister of Australia because the real struggle for the job will begin when the present Parliament is dissolved and only if the Liberal-Country Party coalition is again successful in gaining the Treasury benches.

Another writer thought that giving all contenders **a handwriting test** would sort them out.

In any case, it all went to a vote, and as you have already guessed, **John Gorton won by the length of the straight**.

So, from January 11th, we had a new Prime Minister. He held this post for three years. Billy McMahon was later to succeed him in 1971. John McEwen continued on as Deputy, and as Minister for Trade. He steered Australia through the difficult years where we finally moved our outlook for trade from Britain towards the rest of the world.

Comment. Back in 1967, I encountered John Gorton. I was a Biometrician at the time working in a research position for the NSW Department of Agriculture. I was part of a team that, among other things, was conducting a trial at a Research Station in the NSW town of Condobolin.

It was a trial that was tough on sheep, seeking information on their endurance. We informally called it "our starvation and erosion" trial. In 1967, there was a world conference of Biometricians in Sydney that I attended.

Gorton, as Minister for Science, turned up and moved through the throng shaking hands and being a jolly good fellow. He came across our little group, and asked me what I did, and I gave him the gist of it, including the sheep trial.

A week later, there was a bigger conference for Biometricians in Canberra, with 1,000 delegates crammed into a reception. As I stood there in a group of a dozen people, Gorton was doing his meet-the-scientists routine of shaking hands and offering a token minute of trivial talk here and there. As he squeezed past us, he looked back, and saw me.

He turned, and came into our group, and said "Mr Williams. I want to talk to you." He took me aside, and for the next six minutes, quizzed me thoroughly about the Erosion trial, and the scientists working on it, and just how dedicated they were.

At the end, he thanked me for "my time" and offered me free access to him any time I might want it.

Needless to say, **I was impressed by many aspects of this**. I was quite pleased when he took over the reins as PM.

A DIFFERENT VIEW OF GORTON

Below is a Letter that is probably more typical of how the average voter felt. The person *Ming* mentioned was former Prime Minister Sir Robert Menzies who, before Holt, held the office for 16 years.

Letters, L Coster. The adulation heaped upon the new Prime Minister by certain newspapers would lead one to believe that Alexander the Great had risen from the grave. Actually, the ease with which he won the post points out the deplorable lack of talent among the Liberals sitting in the House of Representatives.

It seems that we are going to have a dose of the "great new society" shoved down our throats, which means, of course, more taxes and more men for Vietnam. I sigh for the days of old Ming, that great White Father who promised us nothing and made sure we got it. At least he ignored us with great dignity, and spared us all the gaff about glorious destinies and exciting tomorrows.

Australians don't abhor dignity. Ming's long term in office proved that. If Senator Gorton or his advisers think that a photograph showing him clad in shorts and leaning on a shovel will endear him to any section of the public, they have another think coming. Australians don't want to be led by a man leaning on a shovel.

Comment. I liked Menzies too, even though I voted against him half the time. What attracted me was that he was so deliberate, and **he thought about things before he talked about them**. At one stage he famously said that if something **political** had reached the stage of urgency, he put the files in a drawer and looked at them a fortnight later. Usually he found that the heat had gone out of them. **Then** he might act.

DEATH IS SO PERMANENT

All States were worried about the death toll on their roads. The NSW Minister for Transport, Milton Morris, reported that the toll for NSW last year was 1,114. He added that while this was distressingly high, it represented a drop of two and a half percent over the previous year. Given the fact that the number of drivers had increased, and that the average driver had travelled more miles, he saw that small drop as a significant turn-around.

Most people thought that the small percentage improvement was just a sampling variation. It could have been the effect of rain or a change in the days on which Public Holidays fell. They thought that Morris needed to do more. Writers to the *SMH* were quite happy to be specific, including fixing the state of the roads and enforcing the existing traffic rules, and making vehicle inspections more rigorous.

A few letter writers came up with **novel ideas**. Fast-moving main road traffic should not be interrupted by cars entering from side streets, one writer said. He argued that these main roads, **called something like expressways**, had priority in many overseas countries, and he could see that a system of expressways across our country areas in particular, would have much merit. **What a novel idea.**

This writer went on to say that death rates could not be reduced "**by gadgets, such as seat-belts.**" Further, he had no use for slogans such as *Death is so Permanent* or *Life is so Precious*. There is no evidence, he went on, that a single person has been saved from death because of a slogan.

A few people picked up on seat-belts.

Letters, W Zech, Publicity Officer, Road Safety Council of NSW. If Eric Marx was really sincere in his attitude towards road safety in his letter he would not have referred to safety belts as "**gadgets.**"

This device adopted for driver and passenger protection surely deserves a better name than "gadget," and if Mr Marx is really serious in referring thus to the safety belt, I am afraid that he is not only ignorant of the great value of the safety belt in reducing the risk of injury to the occupants of a vehicle so fitted, and in many cases of saving lives, but also he is doing a disservice to the cause of road safety itself.

Official surveys made to determine the value of the use of seat belts have proved that **they can reduce the risk of serious injury and even death in some cases by as much as 80 per cent.**

Another writer provided a wealth of statistics that showed that **compulsory** seat-belts had made a big difference, and claimed an improvement of 75 per cent in one case.

He advocated a **nation-wide maximum speed limit of 50 miles per hour on all roads.** Then, he went completely off the rails and advocated **breathalyser tests for motorists** involved in accidents, and random tests for others.

Comment. Of course no true Australian would stand for that. Think of what it would do to the liquor industry.

Comment. Be that as it may, this was a time when the road toll was first coming under real public scrutiny. **The period from 1968 to 1970 (in NSW) was the worst in our history.** After that, the number of dead dropped from 1,114 in 1967 to 380 in 2016.

Official statistics for **2016** show that the three biggest killers were the failure to wear seat belts, alcohol and excess speed. **It seem that our above writers were not all wide of the mark.**

ASIAN NURSES

Many people around Australia were starting to question our adherence to the **White Australia Policy.** Of course, most of them still would not approve of **the Japanese** coming in to this nation as immigrants, but they were ready to accept **other Asians** without much concern. The Government, though, was a bit slower to act. Still, it has now put its toe in the water, and said that it was considering allowing entry of well-qualified school teachers and nurses as "settlers."

Objections flooded in. As one nurse said, Asian girls are willing to work for low salaries under unpleasant conditions, something that our Australian girls are not prepared to do.

Another wrote that Asian girls would be happy to live in sub-standard houses, with poor ventilation and low hygiene.

Comment. These Letters highlight the problem that Government would have in relaxing entry restrictions. **No matter who they brought in**, there were big sections of the community who would oppose them. For example, nurses, as above.

The same would be true for **every profession and trade**. Also, if **unskilled** labor came here, the whole Union movement would rebel. Every section of the workforce could mount opposition to the expected taking of their jobs and lowering of standards.

So, in addition to the talk about **race, blood, colour, customs, hygiene, language, integration, diet, and education,** that normally bedevilled discussion of dismantling the WAP, there was the practical problem *of where do you start?*

THE TENTERFIELD QUINS
Sadly, one of the quins died after four days. According to Wikipedia, in 2017, the other four are still living.

FEBRUARY NEWS ITEMS

Stock Exchanges round the nation are suspecting that a boom in mining shares is imminent. Shares in Western Mining Corporation today jumped to $53, up $10. BHP closed at a record high. All mining shares, no matter what they were seeking or producing, joined in the Gold Rush.

The biggest issue dividing Australian society was our **involvement in Vietnam.** Half the nation said we should be fighting there, and the other half said we should withdraw....

One of **Gorton's first decisions** was announced when he said that **we would not increase the total number of troops there.** Prior to this, we had added more troops every time the US asked for more help. **It was an open cheque**....

Now, Gorton said the number would be frozen. This did not satisfy the withdrawers fully, but it at least **froze our level of involvement**.

There is a crisis at Sydney's Taronga Park Zoo. A tiger snake has given birth to 22 babies. This is well above the average litter. There is a thus a shortage of frogs and skinks that can be used to feed them.....

The Zoo is offering to buy these "morsels." They must be very small because the reptiles themselves are only four inches in length.

The **famous pop group, the Bee Gees**, have landed a $1 million contract to tour the US. You will remember that **two of them are Australian**, and **the three other brothers migrated here as children...**

Have you ever seen the **Australian film** *Smiley*. I bet you do not know that the title role was played by **Australian-born Colin Petersen, the Bee Gees drummer.**

Several reports come in **every day about the US victories in Vietnam.** Today, one of them talked about **800** enemy troops attacking a US position, and **122** were killed. "**One American was killed**, and 20 wounded"....

The gross exaggerations in the numbers, coming day after day, was destroying belief that the highly controlled reports coming out of Vietnam **had any basis of fact.**

Jockey George Moore was one of the our greatest Australian jockeys. At a reception for him, he said that Australia should **get rid of bookies from race-tracks.** Other nations, he pointed out, had **only totalisator betting.** These included France, America, and Hong Kong. He said that bookies take too much commission from the takings of racing....

He expected that **before long bookies would be excluded from race tracks in Oz ....**

Over the years, various attempts have been made to do this. **They all failed badly.** Australians did not react well to the thought that they could not go to a track and shop around for the best price. "**Beating the bookie**" was deeply ingrained as an **Australian punter's ideal....**

Not many countries have **both** on-course bookmakers and TABs.

WAR IN VIETNAM

I have given you some material on Vietnam already, but I need to enlarge on that to give you a better picture. So, I will talk about that war for most of this Chapter. After that I will only touch on the subject here and there, when something particularly disturbing happens. But I will ask you to remember at all times that this dirty war was being fought all day every day, and that our boys were there and being killed and maimed. Remember too that it would go on for another four years, and that it would end with the US (and Australia) pulling out with their tails between their legs.

TAKING OUR BAT AND GOING HOME

As part of the British decision to go into a form of isolation, it was withdrawing its troops from all over the world. This included Vietnam. So, in the face of much opposition from the US, the Brits took their troops out of that country, and that was that.

America was mightily upset, and preached and sulked and warned. But to no avail. Many in Australia too wanted to follow the British example for various reasons. But they were disappointed. This served to emphasise the now fact that we were no longer part of a protective Empire, but had to find a powerful friend. The USA was starting to look pretty good to us.

SHOOTING OF A PRISONER

The real war in Vietnam had been going on for two years. During that time, our well-known indifference to overseas events left us relaxed and apathetic. After we sent some of our Regular Army troops to fight there, our interest level rose, and so too did the Press coverage. But it was only **when our young boys were selected, and drafted for duty and death there, that the issue became red-hot.**

Since then, half the content of the early pages of the daily Press have been Vietnam related. America sent us copy for the Papers that was free and voluminous and extremely patriotic that we, as good boys and allies, printed and distributed.

Much of this material related to military matters, which I will not generally cover. But occasionally other articles crept through. Here is one such, and it raised quite a storm.

Daphne Lane. Last Saturday, the "Herald" published a photograph of General Nguyen Ngoc Loan, head of South Vietnam's national police, shooting a captured Vietcong prisoner in "cold blood." On Sunday night the film of this incident was shown on Channel 10 News and I can assure you the movie version really brought home the whole scene in vivid and sordid detail.

This policeman calmly walked towards the prisoner without a word or a sign and with not a flicker of feeling, murdered the prisoner. I am surprised that there has not been an uproar in Australia about this act as I always thought that we were noted for our sense of fair play and justice.

In the midst of fighting, one must kill or be killed, I know, but if this General's actions are those that may be attributed to the hierarchy of South Vietnam, then the leaders are little better than the Nazis.

I am sure more sympathy and compassion would have been shown by us to a racehorse, incurably hurt at the course and having to be shot, than that portrayed here.

I had always felt in the past we must fight in South Vietnam to halt aggression and the threat of Communism, but now I am left with one big doubt - are we on the side of the "goodies" or the "baddies"?

Letters, T Welch. The picture in the "Herald" on Saturday of one of our noble allies - a general, no less - shooting a prisoner of war because he had killed Americans and Vietnamese should make us wonder to what sort of people we have given our moral and physical support. Surely the Geneva Convention, on the treatment of prisoners of war, means something to us, even if not to our allies?

This sort of callous treatment of prisoners will only help to make this "dirty war" even dirtier.

This image had such an impact because all we had seen of the war so far was images of the US soldiers (and their allies) fighting to defeat absolute villains, and at the same time, saving the world. **The soldiers were benevolent, and our aims noble.** Now, without any argument, we had seen a brutal act committed by one of the goodies. So, the outrage in this nation was severe.

But not unanimous. Several writers defended the act.

Letters, H Davies. In his righteous indignation, Mr Welch has conveniently overlooked the fact that under the generally accepted Rules of War and the Geneva Convention, any person using arms in a recognised zone of military operations must wear a distinctive uniform and be acting under a lawfully constituted command if he is to be treated as a prisoner of war. If he does not fulfil these two conditions, he can be treated as a "franc tireur" and summarily executed.

The man shown in your picture was certainly not wearing any uniform and I very much doubt if anyone but the Communists consider that the Vietcong is a lawfully constituted body.

In any case, **the man was extremely lucky to have been dispatched so expeditiously. He could have been taken to the rear and tortured**.

Many responses to this were long and full of military regulations. But this pithy reply was telling.

Letters, H Brownlee. The poor devil who was shot **probably knew nothing** of the Geneva Convention or the Rules of War. He probably had never been issued with a uniform.

But that aside, is Mr Davies saying that if he had had a uniform, he would have been spared. Does that mean that Mr Davies agrees that he **should** have been killed, shot, murdered, because he did not have a uniform.

LET'S GET THIS STRAIGHT

Letters, K Thomas. U Thant has said that in war the first casualty is truth. Amid the contradictory mixture of reports coming from war-torn South Vietnam, the Australian Press deliberately confuses the essential issue by consistently referring to the enemy as "the Communists" or "the Reds."

The fact is that the enemy is the National Liberation Front, of whom only a minority are Communists. Vice-President Humphrey, of the United States, himself said last November that a large proportion of the NLF were not Communists. Martin Luther King has said that American officials know full well that less than 25 per cent of the NLF are Communists. The fact is that they are **patriots, or nationalists, or revolutionaries** - call them what you will but do not deliberately mislead your readers by calling them Reds. Two things are obvious. First, that these Nationalists are putting up the most gallant struggle ever recorded in the history of mankind and secondly that, by being an accomplice to the invasion of the country by 520,000 Americans, Australia is writing the blackest chapter in her history.

Comment. Mr Thomas raises an interesting point, one which a few other **interested** parties are pushing. He is correct in saying that only a minority of the enemy in Vietnam are Communists. He is also correct in implying that they are not fighting to create a Communist State. They are in fact fighting for the independence of their nation, at the same time as 30 other nations around the world are doing the same thing.

But what Mr Thomas is ignoring, for some reason, is that every piece of war-making equipment being used in the war comes from the Reds in Vietnam, or in China, or in Russia. That includes planes and shipping. It includes rifles and artillery, tanks, and flame-throwers. It includes food, clothing and drinks including water. It includes bombs, ammunition and booby traps and land transport. In short, it includes all the apparatus needed to conduct a jungle war. Importantly, it also includes the brainpower and strategic planning that makes an army work.

The Reds are providing all of these. Without these there would be no war in Vietnam, just local groups of armed guerillas struggling in separate bands. Further, right now the number of US troops will start doubling from 500,000 to one million, and so too will the Reds. So that **the locals by then** will be in the minority.

I am not ever a fan of the Press, but on this occasion I must say that, given the above, their use of the term *Red* does not offend me. When a news report says *Red* I know who they are talking about.

Second comment. The well-publicised shooting of the prisoner hit home in America. Most people back there had a Hollywood image of their soldiers talking wistfully about their Mom, and handing out chocolates and silk stockings to simple grateful foreigners. This incident showed that in reality, cruelty existed and, while it did not involve one of their own boys, it compromised their allies.

Doubt was sown by this incident and as the war went on, the American population saw more of these, and worse, including atrocities by some of their own, and later some of them broadcast almost live to their living rooms. At the moment, public opinion on the war was about equally divided, but it could not in the long run stand up to horror evoked by callous events.

GORTON AND THE WAR

Gorton had hardly moved into the Lodge when he said that he would not increase our troop levels in Vietnam. Writers were quick to praise and also condemn him.

Letters, H Davies. Not since Churchill made his famous "We'll fight back" speech in 1940 have I been so moved as when I read the statement by Mr Gorton concerning Australia's future commitments in Vietnam.

After a series of Prime Ministers who either wanted to tie us to Britain's apron strings or to "Go all the way up the garden path with LBJ", it is indeed refreshing that at last we have a leader who is prepared to tell our allies just what we propose to do, and not wait for instructions from London or Washington.

Good on you, Gorton! Here is one vote you may rely on.

Letters, I Scott. I offer no opinion at all on the merits or otherwise of Australia's commitment in Vietnam, but I protest on other aspects of Mr Gorton's statement last Friday. The present circumstances in Vietnam; the timing; the lofty air of finality show it as deplorable.

Crisis developments could occur at any time so to make such dogmatic pronouncements is ridiculous and dangerous.

Mr Gorton should have made no statement at all on this matter at this time.

Comment. The point raised by Scott was valid. Gorton was perhaps unwise to make so emphatic a statement when there was so much uncertainty about the future. Still, it did let the nation know, and America know, that he was definitely not in favour of escalating the war.

WHITHER GOEST THIS WAR

The war was bogged down at the moment. There were of course victories that were proclaimed as historic, little villages saved from the fiends, and brave talk about how soon we would vanquish the evil foe. But we had no easy propaganda victory here, because the Reds were just as good as we were in spelling out these calumnies.

Really, **we were bogged down**. What could anyone do about it? Most people thought we might come to a conference table and negotiate a settlement.

Letters, Sally Meares. We must **not** fall into the trap into which it seems **many of our ideological opponents have already tumbled,** of seeing only a distorted and desperate view of the other side, of seeing "conflict as inevitable, accommodation as impossible, and communication as nothing more than an exchange of threats."

If we, and the United States, realise that basic principles are involved for us, that mistakes have been made on both sides, that there is room for accommodation without abandoning South Vietnam to forceful takeover by a minority, and that the future is ours to make, we will have come a long way towards accepting the need for a negotiated settlement as soon as possible, which is reasonable for both sides. North Vietnam claims she has already reached this conclusion; the only way to prove if she has is to try her. I suggest we do so.

Neither side was ready for this. The posturing and utterances on both sides were too aggressive and full of ideology to allow it. Also, remember that in America (and also Russia) there was a host of industries that made bumper profits from a war. Public opinion can eventually sway America from its path, but the time was not yet ripe.

Negotiating was out of the question. But other extremes were getting more public discussion. One of these was the invasion of North Vietnam by US forces. So far, hostilities were confined to the South. What about giving the North a taste of war on their own soil?

One problem with this was that China would feel threatened, and **this could lead to a catastrophic escalation**.

Letters, Tom Uren, MP. On February 3, 1968, the *SMH* stated that an Assistant Secretary of State forecast a possible United States invasion of North Vietnam - "within a few months."

This strategy has been under discussion for some months by President Johnson's advisers but it seems to me the only restraining influence will be Johnson himself - but in this Presidential election year and with his American boys taking a belting, can he withhold the political pressure of invading the North?

What will invasion of the North mean? It will mean that the United States with the forces at present available **can only invade if they use nuclear weapons**.

Emmet John Hughes, writing in "Newsweek," May 29, 1967, said: "The arithmetic of escalation is beginning to appal. The combined strength of the Vietcong and North Vietnamese regulars exceeds 520,000, of whom less than 115,000 are currently committed to battle. Thus a little more than 20 per cent of enemy forces has sufficed to have US generals clamouring for reinforcement of their army of 440,000."

Even with reinforcements to US forces to over 500,000 - the past week has shown Hughes was not far off the mark. Let us exclude what China may do. What will Russia do if the United States invades the north?

Letters, F James. Continengcy planning for invasion of the Democratic Republic of Vietnam has been a continuing concern of the Pentagon's planning staff for more than two years. One takes it for granted that use of chemical and biological, as well as nuclear, weapons has been considered as a matter of elementary professional military efficiency.

The use of any of these means involves a political decision, not a military one. I am **unaware** of the faintest evidence that President Johnson could conceivably risk using nuclear weapons.

Any invasion of the DRV must accordingly be made with conventional forces and arms. What would this involve? If 1,000,000 US and allied troops cannot contain the military position in the South, then obviously a total of 2,000,000 men will not suffice to subdue the whole of Vietnam, because the DRV has not only large, intact regular forces, but a civilian population which would rise up to a man against the invader.

Ignoring Russian or Chinese reactions (but don't let us forget those 120,000 Chinese troops, at least, who are already in North Vietnam!) where on earth is the US going to find another million men? And, presumably, an additional $26,000 million yearly?

Comment. These latter two writers were prominent politicians, well known for their fiery dispositions, and neither shy of exaggeration. Still, when they spoke they were always listened to, though generally with a small pinch of salt.

Second comment. None of these extremes came to pass. **Negotiations** did go on and on, but both parties were so insincere that they got nowhere. **The invasion of the North was too dangerous.** The lobbyists for **nuclear, chemical biological weapons**, quite powerful in the USA, were kept at bay.

So the war ground on. **And on.** In the long run, hostilities ended when enough sensible Americans said they had had enough. If you do not remember the results, I will save more comment on them till later in this book. But I will give you a hint. **Do not look for peace much before 1972.**

QUICK QUESTION ON VIETNAM

A writer asked a valid question.

Letters, L Douglas. Twenty years after this shocking war is over, how will the indigenous people of Vietnam judge **who were the worst villains of the war?** Those who were born in Vietnam (no matter what part of it) **or** armed troops from other lands having no ethnical relationship to the peoples of Vietnam?

MARCH NEWS ITEMS

Lionel Rose, a young Aboriginal boxer, won the **World Featherweight Title**. He was **welcomed** at Melbourne's airport by 5,000 people and at the Town Hall **by 10,000**. These crowds were about the same as President Johnson got about a year earlier.

Waverley Council **reflected the more accommodative attitude to Aborigines** by starting a scheme which aims to send an Aboriginal student boy (and girl) to Waverley College each year. **The bursary will pay all fees and boarding costs.** Waverley is a Municipality in Sydney's select and expensive Eastern Suburbs, a long way from Aboriginal land. The School is also a high quality CHS school....

Even if all other things were unchanged, **the Council Board would not have thought of this 10 years ago**. In this social aspect at least, **times are changing fairly rapidly**.

Nurses in NSW (and other States) have received **a new award that increases their wages**. It also gives them **two days off per week** rather than the **previous one and a half days**. Also, an allowance for split shifts. As one commentator put it, the new award **brought them out of the Dark Ages and into the Middle Ages**.

A helicopter with a TV crew on board flew out from Alice Springs, loitered over Ayers Rock, **then fell from the sky and crashed onto the Rock**. It came to rest "on the brink of the southern end of the Rock, which is 1,100 metres high". No one was hurt.

Rhodesia is a **British nation** in Africa where colonialists have ruled for a century. Like a host of other nations, **its native population wants to become independent.** Two years ago, some of its ruling bodies proclaimed that they were indeed independent, and the matter was currently confused and being discussed fervently....

Three men were recently sentenced to death there. The Queen reprieved them. But the hangings went ahead, in defiance of Britain. This may lead to **the final break between Rhodesia and Britain.** In any case the **ruling white majority will be feeling very uneasy** for themselves and their considerable land holdings and farms. **We will hear more about this as we proceed.**

Three Super-Powers, the **USA, Britain and Russia**, have put forward **a Plan to offer protection against nuclear attack to all nations of the world.** In return, countries **would have to forsake their own development** of nuclear arms....

Anyone with a brain in his head can immediately **see a dozen reasons why this is a silly Plan.** For example, the French President, de Gaulle, fearing a ground attack from Russia or the USA, is thinking of establishing **nuclear** sites in the **Pacific** that will launch bombs if their existing home bombs are disabled. **This was announced on the same day as the above Peace Plan....**

But taken **with** the useless efforts of the UN to get a solution in Vietnam, **the world was giving up on listening** to the various international bodies that talked and talked and achieved nothing.

WELCOME TO THE CLUBS

NSW has just held an election, and the incumbent Premier, Bob Askin, and his Liberal Party, easily retained their control. Askin had made an election promise that he would change the Law to allow persons over 18 to use Clubs. The previous Law had set a higher age limit of 21.

When he announced the new limit, he got some criticism. A few people had a perennial dislike of clubs and the demon drink, and saw this as just a further expansion of their influence. Some Churches said that their evils would now be multiplied and spread to younger age groups. Some saw it as a money grab by the clubs because youths and girls would pour in to play the pokies.

Others thought that youth would be lured from healthy outdoor, wholesome activities into smoke-filled gambling dens. One lady said that she would support the measure for any Club that hired a social worker who would help the youngsters who were certain to run astray.

But their arguments did not have much community support.

Letters such as the one below stopped most arguments in their tracks. This was written in January, a month before the change of the Law.

Letters, Returned Veteran. The Army took me away from my studies, and gave me training. Also they gave me a gun, a uniform and a kit-bag. They sent me off to Vietnam and after a while I shot and killed a few 15-year-old lads, and had my ankle blown off by a booby trap. Then I came back and have almost recovered at home.

I find that when I want to go in the evenings after tea to a Club, with my Mum and Dad for a quiet talk, that I can't, because I am too young.

I was able to go to my horrible fate in Vietnam, fight and kill for my country, but not to the local Club.

Comment. It is hard to argue with that and similar Letters. In any case, Askin brought down the legislation, with very little resistance.

QUESTIONS FOR THE ARMY

Our Army is in hot water. An American journalist, not famed for his balance or accuracy, has just released a book on the Vietnam war. In it, he describes how officers and men, in one of our Units in Vietnam at a place called Nui Dat, gave water torture to a girl prisoner. Apparently, a military investigation was held at the time and found no problems and no official document was made public.

With the release of the book, several persons, including some civilian witnesses, have stated that the torture did happen, and there are allegations floating round that other examples might be revealed.

All of this has disturbed our comfortable view of our troops overseas. Like the Americans, we have clung to the idea that our troops are always good, and that the enemy is always bad. But maybe that is not the case.

Several writers had their say.

Letters, A Blackshield. In an "open line" program on a Sydney radio station last Friday night, an Australian soldier telephoned to say that in his experience, such torture is in fact a regular part of the Australian forces' conduct of their role in Vietnam. What made his statements appalling was that they were offered not by way of confession, but in purported explanation of the "reasonableness" of what allegedly occurred at Nui Dat. Instead of complaining of "atrocity," said the speaker, we should take it for granted that this is the only way to treat Asians.

After the initial attempts at suppression of Mr Sorell's story, it was disturbing that this latest statement appeared to be given no publicity in any section of the Saturday Press. The speaker's attitude may or may not be widespread among Australian soldiers; his account of their behaviour may or may not be true. But we need to **know**, not just to **assume**.

Can we now be assured that the whole matter will be exhaustively and **publicly** explored by the proposed military court of inquiry - or, better still, by some independent body whose findings we might feel able to believe?

Comment. You can see Mr Blackshield's reluctance to believe what he heard. Though deeply shocked, he doubted whether the attitude was widespread, or true. **He needs to know, not assume.** He wants a full exhaustive and public enquiry, not by the Army, but an independent body. **This was an attitude that was common to most Australians.**

The next day, anyone who had wavered would have been joined by more when the next Letter appeared. It is a bit garbled at times, but the writer's point is obvious.

Letters, Serving Soldier. I'd like to comment on this torture rubbish.

What a song and dance about a trivial incident! I know of an incident when the Vietcong cut a pregnant woman open, and left her hanging, still alive, in front of our troops. Then cut two men down, who tried to rescue her. This never even reached the papers.

If this form of torture is used, so what? It's merely child's play when compared with the methods that the VC use. It's easy to judge, back here in Australia, it's easy to judge when you are in base areas in Vietnam. You can be as self-righteous as you like. Things change, though, when all you have between you and eternity is a rifle, and your senses. When you have to go out and kill the enemy. When you have to patrol through the jungle, and your next move could be your last. Why don't you leave the Digger alone to fight the war? Why do you have to interfere and tip the balance more in favour of the Vietcong?

We're fighting a war! We're fighting it as fair as we can, and the Vietcong fight dirty, but we get all the knocks. Nobody kicks if the VC torture anybody.

The information that girl had would have been important.

So long as we fight the war the way the journalists want it, all will be well. The VC? Well it doesn't matter what they do!

Comment. We all have to be careful reading Letters, because we are never certain they contain the truth. But if we suppose that this person is in the Fighting Forces, and this Letter reflects his view and that of his colleagues, then our view of the integrity of our troops must suffer.

Then there was this from a different angle, but tacitly admitting the torture.

Letters, M Crawley. I have no doubts that the Government deplores the actual practice of brutal and inhumane treatment by our own members of Australian military forces. I doubt if many of our men would, in fact, be prevailed on to use such means. But if we can accept these methods by our allies, where does this fine distinction leave us? Too many of our people are being torn apart by these issues and there is an ever-increasing number of us who feel that if this is to be the price we pay for economic benefits or shelter under the American defence umbrella, then we just cannot afford it.

However, one pendulum was swinging the other way.

Letters, Julie Melov. Finally, we have come to this. Now torture is to be considered as inevitable in this monstrous war.

You tell us that we may "burn with shame" over this, but may take consolation in the fact that our Government "will do its best to stop it." The Government MUST stop it. There can be no shade of grey here, it is a strictly black and white issue.

Heaven knows we've condoned napalm, phosphorus, nausea gases, fragmentation bombs and goodness knows what else, but this is as far as we must go.

We must insist that our Government stand totally by its obligations under the Geneva Convention concerning the treatment of prisoners of war, and demand a full and public inquiry into the alleged torture of a prisoner of war. If the Government fails in this fundamental obligation to the people of Australia it cannot expect the people to fulfil any obligations of obedience to such a Government.

Comment. No one could sensibly disagree with Julie Melov's fine sentiments. There will be many who think that, under ideal conditions, it might be possible to fight clean. But there will be just as many, including Vietnam vets, who know that life in war is never like that. The question is not whether you fight dirty, but how far can you go before **your conscience, or some other factor, makes you stop.**

It is a simple matter sitting safely in comfort miles away from Vietnam, and 50 years later, to have opinions about the tortures inflicted by our troops in the war. But until you have sat and talked at length with some of them, you should not get too set in your opinions.

Second comment. You can see how these reports on torture made Australia wonder about the sanctity of our involvement. But, taking a longer term view, such events gradually piled up, one after the other, and each of them made a small part of the population waver in their support for the war. And, as I said earlier, this number was starting to grow, ever so slowly, until it was a major force that had to be reckoned with.

Third comment. Without giving the game away, I should say that **the evils committed by our allies in the war grew over the years to the stage where major scandals erupted in the home nations concerned**. Happily, Australia was not one of these nations.

YOU ARE OPERATING ON MY TURF

I was born in 1934 in a house in a place I called home in the small coalmining town of Abermain. My mother was assisted by one of the town's two midwives, and she was the same one who had assisted at the birth of my **eldest** brother 15 years earlier.

My **elder** brother made his entrance a different way. He was born in 1931, and this was on the tail-end of the Depression and the Lock-out. So there was no pay for miners for two years, and so to literally survive, my family moved to the shores of Lake Macquarie where they camped for 20 months in an old military tent, and lived off fish, rabbits, and the vegetables that they grew.

My brother was born in the midst of this. So he was born not at home but in a tent. My mother was this time assisted by adjacent campers wives. If things had got complicated, in my case, a doctor would have been available after surgery next day. In my brother's case, no doctor would visit the campers.

Let me skip forward to 1968. At a birth in my family in 1968, everything happened at a ward in a hospital. A nurse was in and out of the room all the time, the mother was on a drip, an obstetrician was on hand for the birth, and a gynaecologist and other medical specialists were just round the corner. Drugs were available, and even anaesthetic was there as an optional extra. Though I should mention ruefully that dads were not permitted near the scene.

The point I am making is how far the birthing world, and indeed **the entire field of medicine, had come**. Now there was penicillin, X-rays freely available, cures for ulcers, anti-snake venom was in most hospitals, and radiation therapy for cancers. Polio had been cured, and TB mastered. Even the Pill was now a reality, though nothing had been done about the taste to make it palatable to children. **It seemed that the miracles of modern medicine were coming fast and faster.**

Behind the scenes, though, there was much that was unsettling. The Feds, for example, were in conflict as usual with everyone over the implementation of **national health schemes**. And doctors were in conflict among themselves. All the young people who had benefited from

Commonwealth Scholarships in the 1950's were adding to the numbers of doctors, and were trying to find enough turf to operate in.

I will illustrate this by talking about GPs and their role as surgeons. The GP that many of us were brought up with was a family doctor, in a country town or a suburb. Generally as a sole trader, he managed your flu, measles, cuts, heart palpitations, aging, and a million other worries. He also, perhaps twice a week, went to the local hospital, and performed operations on tonsils, broken arms, teeth, and injuries from industrial accidents. In 1965, my local GP did an unsuccessful operation on my father "to cut the cancer out". In general, he was ready to step in and operate as part of his regular routine.

By 1968, medicine was on the move, and this meant that there was **a growing recognition that specialists were needed**. One need was for surgeons, given the same training as GPs, but with additional stress on practical surgery.

As these younger surgeons came into the market, the older GPs were still doing their routine operations.

This first Letter appeared under the *SMH* heading of *Surgery by Amateurs.*

Letters, Surgeon. Many surgical operations performed in this city are done by amateurs, by **surgically untrained doctors who run general practices**.

This incredible situation is encouraged by the fact that the medical benefit payment is the same whether the operator is a GP or a full-time specialist surgeon possessing a higher degree. Consequently GPs are tempted to do surgery for the fee, referring to the specialist often only the public or the obviously complicated patient.

GP surgery is justifiable in the jungle but not here where there are increasing numbers of eager well-trained professional surgeons. The situation must be remedied and could so be done by education of the public to demand the best treatment, reduction of medical benefit payments for GP surgery or legislation against amateur surgery. These measures would immediately result in improved patient care and a reduction in surgical morbidity and mortality.

A few people who responded attacked **the writer**.

Letters, GP. The chances are that "Surgeon" is a young specialist with a high degree and low experience in surgery, frustrated in not getting sufficient referred patients from the GPs. The medical profession has lately, in fact, been plagued by a surplus of these "9 to 5" surgeons, whom the GP naturally mistrusts.

The truth is that because of the ethical and legal barriers, a GP will only undertake an operation he is capable of doing well; anything above it he will refer to a trusted and more experienced surgeon. The less experienced are jealous and greedy for work "come easily"; they will not realise that long years of surgical experience are needed to achieve success.

Many GPs have the confidence, experience and capacity to perform major surgery with no less mortality and morbidity than their colleagues who practise in the same field. No amount of legislation will take away the goodwill, built up over a lifetime of close contact, between a patient and his doctor.

Letters, GP. I would be the first to agree with "Surgeon" that there are many surgeons like him with higher degrees - perhaps young and inexperienced - who feel they can shelter behind their higher qualifications. What he has to realise is that, unlike the more experienced general practitioners, they lack judgment. If "Surgeon" is finding the financial going a little hard, let him get out and do some general practice and earn a name for himself, not expect everything to be handed to him on a platter.

The best safeguard that the public can have is a general practitioner who is guided by his conscience and directs the patient to a specialist whom he knows to be of sound judgment, perhaps not so eager.

Others attacked the **accredited young surgeons as a group**.

Letters, Maurice Ryan.   The possession   of a postgraduate degree does not necessarily make a good surgeon. Fairly recently I witnessed a young surgical registrar in one of our main teaching hospitals performing a major gynaecological operation. Admittedly this was under supervision from a senior surgeon, but the young man's lack of manipulative skill was frightening. He was just plain awkward and, although possibly dedicated, would obviously have been better suited in some less active branch of the profession, perhaps psychiatry.

I also know a well-qualified surgeon who wields the scalpel rather like a tyro country council worker swinging a scythe in long grass.

In the long run probably the situation devolves upon the integrity and morality of the individual GP. Most GPs know their capabilities and their limitations, and are honest enough to act accordingly. Each has a conscience. After all, a GP has, like the surgeon, not only to live with his wife and kids, but with himself.

The GP's did not escape scot free either.

Letters, MB, BS. I heartily agree that many complicated and specialised operations are being performed in this city by general practitioners, many of whom not only lack a higher degree, but also the technical ability which is acquired after years of training in a recognised teaching hospital.

There has for some time been great concern among specialists, who too often inherit the end-results of this butchery, and are invariably called in consultation when it is too late to avert a tragedy. One finds it difficult to believe that in this enlightened, educated community the public can tolerate such a situation and be so credulous as to put their lives into the hands of one of these "amateur surgeons."

Letters, Five Surgeons. This, surely, does not alter the principle that **a proper course of training and testing by examination, as set out by the royal colleges**, should be a prerequisite to the practice of surgery.

Letters, Professional Surgeon. The recent letters from GPs reflect a viewpoint of 20 years ago. One of the reasons for this is, I believe, the persistence of the GP surgeon. Not only by perpetuating mediocre surgery, but more importantly by removing the surgical bread and butter which could keep young surgeons alive while they are making some contribution to surgical progress.

But most writers supported the GPs. I enclose below two short Letters. Both were written by the sons of doctors, The Dads probably thought it was not ethical to respond in their own right.

Letters, Pro GP. My father was a doctor in WWI. He gained his experience as a surgeon in three years on the battle field in France. He would run rings around any surgeon produced in today's teaching institutions.

Letters, Son of Doctor. My father has held a practice in a Victorian country town for twenty years. As a GP, fifty miles from the nearest doctor and hospital, and 200 miles from a specialist surgeon, he has had to conduct many operations. Most of these are routine for him.

If he gets one that is difficult for some reason, he tries to lay it off to the hospital or to a specialist. If he can't, he worries himself sick about it. If he is forced to do it, he dances attendance on the patient until the urgency has passed.

Among the many GPs that I know, patients do not need to worry that the GP will do something capricious or unethical, or beyond their capabilities.

The AMA also threw in its 10 cents worth. With one foot firmly in each camp, it went on to say that accreditation was being looked at by the AMA, and that a pilot trial had been suggested to the NSW Minister for Health.

Comment. You can see that even though every one wrote with restraint and courtesy, the matter was by no means settled. It was a battle that was to **be fought many times in the future as more branches of medicine emerged** with their own claims to independent identities.

If you jump ahead to 2018, you can see that there are many specialties that are flourishing. Most of these are legitimate and completely necessary. But every one of them had some sort of fight in order to be accepted by the medicos and by the public.

The **surgeons,** and the GP's, were about the first to face up to the changes that were about to come.

Second comment. In 2018, GPs have now become gatekeepers for the specialists. They can perform simple procedures and basic diagnosis, but then they reach for the prescription or referral pad. **No longer are there problems with whose turf it is.** They have found their place, and if I might express an opinion, they are filling it very well.

WORDS OF WISDOM

Letters, G Lambert. This being leap year, and having just suffered the imposition of doing an extra day's work on February 29 for which I received no extra wages, I plead for justice.

It will be readily seen that in a normal working life we give 12 days' work free of charge. For this we should be compensated either by the granting of a public holiday on each February 29 or by the payment of double time.

More importantly, perhaps, have you ever considered that the extra day each leap year is making the coming winter later and later? In each 100 years, winter is pushed back over three weeks. Is not this the reason for our changing seasons?

Will we live to see our grandsons playing cricket in the winter and football in the summer?

Letters, Greta Cody. That is every year, at daylight saving start, the authorities take away one hour of sleep, and so on for about 150 days. That means by the end, we are owed about 150 hours of sleep.

They then give us back one miserable hour. So we end up with a sleep deficit of 150 hours. Over 60 years, this adds to 9,000 hours.

No wonder old people are tired.

THE DREADED BREATHALISER

This device is surely coming to everyone. You can see below that it has risen to the stage where we need to send bodies overseas to study it.

Letters, K Davis. We read in the "Herald" that the NSW Commissioner for Motor Transport, Mr D Coleman, will visit England for three months to make "an on-the-spot assessment of the effectiveness of breathalysers."

Three months in England, when Western Australia, Tasmania, South Australia and Victoria **have already introduced breathalyser tests!**

By making an **interstate visit of a couple of days** could not the Commissioner obtain first-hand information on the subject, particularly relating to Australian conditions?

Comment. These wonderful perks, of months overseas, were now common for government employees, and all sorts of agencies and, sometimes, half the local Council.

It was hard for Joe Blow to protest because the ring-leader in the overseas jaunts was Bob Menzies. He had been Prime Minister until two years ago, and in his sixteen years in office, he had had one major trip almost every year. Then he would parade in the highest places in London, and generally flit through America on return. Though his flitting was generally done on a liner, so that meant he was often away, from the land he loved and governed, for two months at a time.

Given that example, lesser mortals could but follow.

APRIL NEWS ITEMS

The **Nazi Party** is attempting to **make political headway** in all cities around Australia. In Brisbane, it attempted to hold its first Sunday afternoon gathering in Centennial Park. The **members turned up with Nazi flags and swastika** armbands, but were met by **200 Jews who tried to punch the living daylights out of them**. They fled. The meeting lasted eight minutes.

On April 6th, Dr Martin Luther King was assassinated in Memphis in the United States. King was the recognised **leader of the Black Civil Rights movement**, and, as a clergyman, **preached non-violent resistance to racial discrimination**. In this capacity he had earned the respect of both blacks and whites....

Serious rioting broke out on his death, in negro regions across the nation, and places like New York and Florida were badly affected. Riots continued for a fortnight and in some places it was said that civil war might break out.

The world's largest passenger liner, *the Queen Elizabeth*, has been sold to an Philadelphia business syndicate. It will be moored in the Delaware River, and used as **a hotel, restaurant, convention venue and holiday resort**.

The New Zealand ship, *Wahine*, **sank in Wellington Harbour. 51 people are reported dead.** There were 600 passengers and 130 crew aboard. The ship had attempted to enter the harbour during a severe gale, and crashed onto rocks. In early morning light, it toppled over on its side, and lay there mostly submerged. Many frantic passengers dived into the icy waters, while a fleet of vessels came to their rescue....

There were five Australians among the dead.

A Vatican specialist said, after studying the *Holy Shroud*, that **Jesus Christ had a height of 5 feet 4 inches.** He was two inches taller than the average Jew at the time.

A man in Western Australia was **sent to gaol for six months** for having **stolen a Diners Club credit card and running up a bill of $2,000.** This is **a new type of crime in Australia,** and came under the category of fraud.

Japanese car sales in Australia were 13 per cent of the total sales in February, and were on a steep rise. Ford had 23 per cent, and Holden 27. Both of the latter were falling. **The war with Japan is well and truly over.**

Evangelist Billy Graham is back in Sydney, drawing a crowd of 60,000 to the Sydney Cricket Ground. A total of 2,8791 persons came forth and "acknowledged Christ." This is Graham's second campaign here. The **previous tour was enormously successful** in attracting numbers. **It was not clear if he had any lasting effect.**

This Sunday afternoon, **the Nazi supporters turned up in the Sydney Domain. Dressed in brown uniforms,** they were pelted with tomatoes, and were soon escorted by the arms from the scene by police....

Their efforts to recruit members were not succeeding at the public level, but **they did collect a number of odd bods who remained active, but no threat,** for another dozen years.

BILLY IS BACK

Billy Graham arrived back in Australia for a repeat of his successful tour of 1959. He brought with him a plane-load of workers who would stage his productions, and another plane-load of equipment and paraphernalia for staging the extravaganza.

Here in Australia, he recruited 1,000 volunteers who would help at the 10 gatherings he would hold. He had already set up agreements with the Protestant Churches as to who would pay for the tour. Also, that those Churches would whip up their congregations so that big crowds would be guaranteed. He then presented, as the complete showman, to meetings of always 10,000 or more, and as the highlight, he always got over 100 people to come forward for a special blessing and to proclaim their faith.

When I write in the matter-of-fact style above, it misses **the excitement that these events produced. People were excited by the event itself.** The loud jazzy religious music on arrival, the singing before-hand, the lighting on the stage, the triumphant entry of Billy Graham, the sometimes fiery presentation of his message, with choirs of pretty young people looking so sincere. Then came the individual proclamations and the wild applause as they came forward, and the final exit with the choirs and organ grinders giving a satisfying farewell. **What a grand spectacle.** Well worth the money, especially **given that it was all free.**

As well as that, there was **another type of excitement that some people, in fact many people, felt.** That was the excitement of being close to their God. Of being with a horde of other people who also were close to God. It was the excitement that comes from realising once again that God is part of your life, and that **his** mission is **your** mission. For those thousands of casual church attendees who accepted the Graham message, the revival of their fervour was an enlightenment.

Prosaic matters always intervene. Observers of these activities had different opinions. Some of them were rapt, and were wholesome in promoting God's word.

Letters, Ola Dickinson, Mosman Baptist Church. The "Herald's" factual reporting of the Billy Graham Crusade has been much appreciated. This "happening" in Sydney will affect the lives of many hundreds of young people, as any demonstration of such magnitude inevitably does.

What spilled a steady flow of people into the arena of dedication and personal commitment in front of Billy Graham's rostrum?

There are those who will say that it is personal magnetism, mass hypnosis through a strong and attractive personality. But many people in the higher tiers of distant stands could hardly have seen the preacher, let alone his eyes and the expression of his face!

Was it high-pressure evangelism with a strong appeal to the emotions? We have **seldom heard preaching so little calculated to stir the emotions**. Sports contests stir greater emotional displays than Billy Graham did at the Showground.

What was it then? What brought the steady tramp of hundreds, thousands of feet, toward the podium - towards Jesus Christ - night after night in the earthy atmosphere of the Showground of modern Sydney?

It was the Holy Ghost! We have seen Him at work in Sydney, and believe that many people have come into closer touch with God through this "happening" at the Showground, and that Sydney will never be the same again because of it.

Letters, David W Sloane. Mr Graham would be the first to point out it is not his salesmanship or magnetic personality that draws people out to accept Christ. It is the spirit of God working in the hearts and minds of people.

Others rejoiced because of God's effect on mankind.

Letters, B Douglas. The Rev Coughlan's "A cool look at Billy Graham" prompts me to say how thankful I am for the sake of our country and the world, that so many thousands admit their "failures," "guilt and inability to cope with life's problems" and have expressed their desire to "accept Christ - decide for Christ, repent, believe, obey."

Our world is in the mess it is in today because men have, on the whole, rejected God as the "Supreme Authority."

Some others complained that Graham's message was too much like Bible History taught in Sunday Schools. Or that it was full of admonitions to be a "jolly good fellow", and love thy neighbour and "all that rubbish." Or that it talked about the **New** Testament Bible and love from God, and ignored the **Old** Testament God of wrath and vengeance. Or that there was no mention of Theology, instead just a "collection of platitudes from the *Womens' Weekly.*"

A few people complained that Graham took it for granted that everything in the Bible was true. There was a response to that assertion.

Letters, (Rev) Harry Bates. If by "A cool look at Billy Graham" the Rev W Coughlan means an impartial look, the article is a failure. Much of the writer's assessment is fair, but the sting is in the tail when **he says**, "The Graham version of the Gospel rests squarely on the assumption that the whole Bible is infallibly (and literally) true... (and) many people blessed (or cursed) with inquiring minds cannot accept this version of the Gospel."

This leaves the false impression in the mind of the reader that the Bible cannot stand the test of linguistic (Hebrew, Aramaic and Greek) scholarship and careful, critical research.

Mr Coughlan fails to tell his readers, what is common knowledge among trained ministers, that there is an **evangelical school of thought, supported by advanced scholarship**, which fully subscribes to biblical theology as expounded by Billy Graham.

Quite a few writers questioned the cost of the series, and asked what other way might there be.

Letters, W Dorey. My personal opinion is that this crusade is a colossal business undertaking costing thousands upon thousands of dollars to run, and enjoyed by a large number of paid employees who travel the world under ideal conditions preparing the way for Billy Graham, who in turn follows them around - also under ideal conditions.

He is a genius at getting his listeners all worked up on the spur of the moment, but is it lasting?

Letters, John Bray. In your report of Billy Graham's meeting on Sunday it is stated that Bishop Kerle explained that the crusade expenditure amounted to $212,000, of which more than half had already been subscribed by "interested Christian people."

This money subscribed for and spent on high-powered American salesmanship, aimed mainly at already Christian folk, is equivalent to the gross total earnings in one year of well over 100 Anglican priests or Protestant ministers.

For this money, these clerics will each average up to 100 sermons or more and will administer the various sacraments and rites of their respective Churches for a full year.

In addition they will assist the poor, counsel the sick, comfort the dying, console the bereaved, teach the young, and carry out numerous other good works known only to God and themselves.

"Interested Christian people" should reflect carefully whether their money would not be more profitably spent on local ministers of the Gospel rather than overseas evangelists.

Having said all that, it is safe to say that 90 percent at least of those who attended came away more than satisfied.

But now the question was raised by others. **Did the effects wear off in time? Were the wonders worked simply one-day wonders?**

After Graham's last visit, these questions were asked time and again. All sorts of committees and interested parties did studies here and abroad to find answers. The results came loud and clear. **Church bodies** found that the effects were long-lasting. **Other bodies** found they were ephemeral, and fleeting. So, the result was indeed quite clear. That is, **you could not trust any party that had a vested interest in the matter.**

Personal Comment. I read carefully the transcript of Graham's speech, and found it in no way exceptional. It went for 50 minutes, in fact, too long, and said no more that the average Anglican clergyman on an average Sunday.

Still, there is no doubt that thousands came away inspired. I would be silly and out of my depth if I commented on why this was so, and I will not comment on whether it had a lasting effect.

I will ask the question, though, on whether such a campaign **should be judged** on how long its effect lasted. Is one year a good result? Ten years? Till death? Maybe, for a few hours might be a good result. Like a good movie.

In any case, if you see **the official statistics**, and if you talk to many who attended, the whole circuit was a great success. Perhaps he will come back again in another 10 years. Just as a spectacle, if nothing more, he would be welcome.

JAP JOBS

Our Trade Minister, "Black" Jack McEwen, liked having our own car industry. Over the last 20 years, locally produced Holden and Ford, and more recently Chrysler, had gained 50 per cent of the local market between them. This brought capital into the country as these American companies gradually expanded. It also brought in more capital as we sold some of them overseas. On top of that, McEwen could see that we needed a local car industry in case war came again, and we were then cut off from overseas suppliers.

So, with the import of Japanese cars growing so quickly, he decided to raise tariff on these vehicles to a massive 45 per cent. By raising their price paid in Australia by so much, he hoped to protect the local industry.

Reaction was a bit mixed, but most motorists could not see the funny side of this.

Letters, R Swinburn. The growing import of Japanese cars has recently reared its ugly head. The Minister for Trade and Industry, Mr J McEwen, has indicated he will take steps to protect Australian manufacturers. And an official inquiry has been instigated.

However, as the owner of a Japanese car, I feel many people are losing sight of the facts amid a ground swell of sentimentality. The brutal fact is, despite an import duty of 45 per cent, the Japanese cars offer better finish, greater safety and in short are better value than their Australian-made or assembled counterparts.

Let the powers-that-be investigate the engineering standards of locally made products. **Make them offer a product equal in quality to their imported opposition.**

To raise import duties further or provide some other extra protection would only hit one person - the buyer.

And isn't this the free enterprise Government?

Letters, N Gould. Before the Government rushes into higher tariffs or voluntary restrictions on Japanese imported cars at the request of the Australian motor industry, perhaps it would be better for the industry to examine its own product.

Do we, as the consumer, require the oversize models being thrust upon us by the "big three" (Ford, GM-H, Chrysler). What was wrong with the 2 to 2 1/2 litre compact of four years ago? (EH Holden, XP Falcon, etc?)

The current models, which were originally introduced into this market for the average working Australian, are now far beyond his means. Prices have risen, petrol consumption has increased, tyre life has decreased, parking both at home and in our all too limited parking areas has become a problem.

Until these firms realise that the Australian motorist does not want to be "Americanised" by the introduction of bigger and bigger models, the inroads being made into their sales by the Japanese compact will further increase.

The NRMA recently did a survey to establish the requirements of the public in their ideal car. Why can't the manufacturers follow suit and produce what we want?

Letters F Arditto. The history of Australian motor manufacture has been a sorry one - nothing new has ever been produced, nor has design kept up-to-date. Economy of operation has gone by the board, and the body rust problem has not been looked at by "The Big Three", much less eliminated. The oversized American-designed cars show considerable body rust long before hire-purchase payments are finalised.

Letters, Jill Kerr. If Australian car manufacturers were to plough back some of their enormous profits into improving their product and lowering their price, I suggest that they would have less to fear from Japanese competition.

Letters, John K Lambeth. If Australian motor vehicles are so inferior that they cannot compete in Australia against imported vehicles with up to 45 per cent loading, how can our cars ever expect to compete with vehicles in foreign countries?

If the Government wants to give assistance it should liven up the industry to build cars that Australians want, not to put up a higher wall for it to hide behind.

Letters, G Ferris. The Japanese are hard-working, efficient and capable and, because of their larger production runs, lower wages and fewer holidays, are able to produce goods at lower costs than we can in Australia. Without tariff protection, most of our secondary industries just could not compete on the local market. But with all the goodwill we can offer, we cannot allow our own industrial development and employment opportunities to be frustrated and ultimately destroyed.

Letters, F MacDiarmid. There is no point in creating jobs for Australian workers producing "57 varieties" of cars, if the resultant products are too costly for those same workers, as consumers, to buy.

There was also talk about the Japanese **dumping** their cars in Australia. This means selling vehicles for less than the cost of production. Most Trade Treaties forbade this, but there were plenty of accounting tricks that allowed it to be done. No one paid much real attention to charges of dumping.

Letters, Philip Ashton. Figures supplied by the Commonwealth Statistician, January-June, 1966, show that Australia exported 1,959 motor vehicles at an average price of less than $1,390.

Those prices sound very low compared with what we have to pay on the local market.

Could it be that, right under the nose of the Minister for Trade, Australia has been dumping cheap cars on the export market?

Comment. The Jap cars kept coming in.

BLACK SPOTS AROUND THE WORLD

Martin Luther King was the spokesperson for the blacks in America. Despite the fact that he was a fierce and moving orator, his moderate and gradualist approach had gained him the respect of white leaders. On his death, much regretted by all, many other leaders of black resistance movements unleashed their black people power onto the streets, and causing riots and disruptions across the nation.

This was a world where there were dozens of other nations whose black minorities were also fighting for equality for themselves. They looked to the USA for any lessons that could be learned, or any opportunities that might come their way.

In Australia there was little reaction to the US events. Only a few Letters made it into the columns of the *SMH*. **The first of these** was a moderate piece that ended with a vague threat to stability, but was barely a shadow of the violence and upheaval promised in the American Press.

Letters, David Cleaver. The Negro feels he has been lied to and tricked for a century; that promises of gradual recognition were false and insincere. Technology provides him now with omnipresent evidence of the wealth of "his" country, which he is denied. He demands his share of the wealth; more, he demands, right now, fulfilment of the deferred promises of a century, centring upon one all-important question, the right of brotherhood.

There have been those in the establishment who, relying on traditional Negro patience, counselled, generation after generation, a gradual advancement of the Negro; so gradual indeed that the Negro came to feel the reverse was happening. If some of these were insincere, it is now, at any rate, too late. Time has run out and the Negro will accept no half-measures in his present feeling of outrage, humiliation and despair.

The authorities will use force, coupled with accelerated welfare-State programs to stave off revolt. They can offer much, but they cannot offer brotherhood. I fear they will not succeed.

A second Letter switched over to South Africa and its apartheid policy of segregation of blacks and white, with the suggestion that this would work in the USA.

Letters, M Aronsen. The solution might be found by following in a modified fashion the policy of South Africa. There must be in the vast area of the United States, some part of some State, not by any means a wilderness, that could support a Negro population of up to 30 million people. **Let this area be given to the Negroes.**

The US Government could well afford to bear the cost of finding suitable homes and land for the displaced white population. The US Government could also allocate a few thousand million dollars to start the Negro on the way to build a future for himself. Let him learn self-government on his own and not rely on others to help him.

This idea was squashed pretty quickly.

Letters, (Miss) J Otton. Civil rights does **not** mean placing the Negro in **a group out of the white man's sight and conscience**, but treating him as a human being, giving him the same rights and opportunities as a white man, and letting him be **free to live where and how he wants**. It's because the white man doesn't observe these basic requirements that the Negro riots. He's not doing it for fun. No one will listen to his peaceful demands, so all he can do is force people to listen.

Turning to Australian Aborigines, one writer expressed his fears, while another asked a few questions.

Letters, J Dalton. It is to be hoped that those advocates of the abolition of the White Australia policy are viewing with horror, revulsion and disgust the events in the

United States of America, following the assassination of Dr Martin Luther King.

God forbid that the same thing should one day happen in this fair country of ours.

Letters, Ben Halstead. While the papers are carrying the agony of the Negro-white crisis in the United States, it would be timely to look at our own position. Could we ask these questions of ourselves?

Are the mass of Australian whites ignorant of the Aboriginal situation, or do they ignore it? How often is the phrase "It's not a matter of colour, but a matter of hygiene" used, and can we afford to generalise? Is there prejudice in employment in our own towns and cities? To our knowledge, in Armidale, there is only one Aboriginal shop-assistant. Do they not apply for these positions? Are we doing enough to sort out their problems of education and housing? Do the whites make an effort to fit the Aboriginal in, or does he have to push in?

In fact, is our record any better?

Comment. I think that Mr Halstead might be surprised by the answers he got. Right now, Australians were voting solidly for changes, all over the nation, that affected Aboriginal citizenship, and gave them greater rights. Granted, there was, and is, still a long way to go, but the change in attitude in the 1960's was remarkable. The last few years of the Sixties were truly the starting point for acceptance of Aborigines by the bulk of whites.

The well-known and much respected advocate for Aboriginal affairs, Michael Sawtell commented. "Charles Perkins said recently that our Aborigines might be so excited by the riots in the US that they would riot themselves. This is rubbish, Aborigines never riot."

MAY NEWS ITEMS

May 1st. The **NSW Government** announced that many of its **controls over most rents would be abolished** from January 1st next year. This will mean that about 50,000 tenants, **who have not had their rent increased since 1940**, will now be **forced to pay full market price** for living in their homes....

This marks the end of a **period of great injustice to landlords**. I will give more details in the body of the text.

The NSW Police have decided that it will have a new emergency number. It will be 000, and will now be consistent with similar numbers for Emergency and Fires....

But remember that **these numbers were then dialed, not pushed.** And remember that **0** was the last digit on the dial. So to dial **000** required three full turns of the dial....

Many people suggested that the number 111 would be better.

Four **reporters, three of them Australian**, were **shot to death in a jungle in Vietnam**. They were in a jeep, and were not armed. As they came to an oil-drum road-block, they called out "Reporters, Reporters", but the Vietcong were not convinced, and opened fire.

Robert Kennedy, the brother of the slain President of the USA, **has won his first Democratic primary.** Voters in the State of Indiana elected him by a comfortable margin....

Could this become the start of a **new dynasty of two, and then three, Presidents all named Kennedy in US politics**? Many pundits are betting on it.

The Federal Government has put **a tariff of 45 per cent on the importation of Japanese cars**. But that has not stopped large numbers from flooding into the nation. So now it has "persuaded" **Japanese manufacturers to increase the price by an average of $200 per car Will this stop the flow? ...**

The new prices **will not take effect for about a month**. So, right now, there is **a great stampede** for new Jap cars right across the nation.

1,200 American servicemen will be on R and R leave in Sydney this week. There is nothing unusual about this. They come regularly after a stint of some months in Vietnam...

But **there will be another 1,200 foreigners here** as well. **These will be Russians, and they are not troops.** They are seamen with **the Russian whaling fleet**, stationed in the Antarctic, and have been at sea for nine months....

Russia is playing no part in fighting in the Vietnam war, and it is expected that there will be no conflict between the two sets of visitors....

In fact, **great conviviality was shared by both the Capitalists and the Communists....**

At this time, **Australia was not worried by the Japs and Russians** taking whales. In fact, we were still doing what we could to have our own whaling industry. **Greenies had not yet become a cohesive force.**

THE WAR IS OVER - MAYBE

In 1940, when the threat of invasion by the Japanese was at its highest, the Government moved all available manpower and resources into military purposes. This meant that our building industry was denuded, and the construction of dwellings came to a halt. The Government thought at the time, probably rightly, that it had better freeze all rentals otherwise a massive inflation would have added to our worries.

So, that's what all States and the Commonwealth did. Between them, they froze rents on dwellings and business premises for the duration of the War. *Whacko,* thought the tenants, no rent rises for quite a while. Landlords saw it differently, but hoped that the War would soon be over.

So, peace came in 1945. But some Clever Dicks in the Government decided that the War was not over until we formally signed a peace Treaty with Japan. **That happened in 1951.** You might expect **then** that rent controls would be lifted. But you would be wrong. A different set of Clever Dicks, our politicians, knew that rents should have been rising quickly with inflation, and that renters were on a great wicket with rents fixed at 1940 values. And they knew that if they threatened to raise rents, **vast hordes of renters would vote against them**.

So, all States, and their Federal counterparts, devised **all sorts of rules and devices to stop rises in rents. For example**, they said some landlords **could** get increases. **All they needed to do** was hire a lawyer and perhaps a barrister, make complex applications to remote public servants in the big cities, wait for months and years, appear before a Court, perhaps appeal the decision, and then they **might** get a judgement in their favour.

But only if the Court thought that the tenant could afford the increase, or only if the landlord had made **capital** repairs to the property. **Not running repairs.** In short, the process of getting a rent rise was a gamble that was costly, and fraught with difficulty and disappointment. Most landlords never chanced it.

So the landlords battled on throughout the 1950's. Early in the 1960's, South Australia and Victoria started to change their laws to produce a fairer deal, and by late 1968, the laggard NSW got on the bandwagon. The changes came in dribs and drabs, as various States did their own thing.

Still, by 1968, **landlords** could look forward to a period when their properties could be rented at a fair market price. That period from 1940, 28 years of it, had been hard on them, and no one could say that it had been fair. One benefit that they received was that when the blessed days arrived, the value of their properties showed a big rise, because now at last they could earn a decent return on their investment.

As for a backlash on the politicians who revised the laws, they got off lightly. By now, for the bulk of the population, the shortage of housing was the main problem. **Some** among them **might cry out against rent increases**, but there was little sympathy in society for them after their period of almost free-loading, and their voices were lost among the larger numbers who were happy to welcome the re-birth of the rental housing and commercial market.

THE ARMY FOR SOME

As the scope of the Vietnam war grew, we realised that we could not play our part unless we found more troops. As usual, we devised various ways to put this burden on the shoulders of very young men. So, theoretically, the birthdays of all 20-year-olds were picked from a barrel, and if his birthday was drawn out, then that young man put his troubles in his kit bag and off he went to the war.

A lot of youths did not like this for a variety of reasons. **One group**, called conscientious objectors, said that they had an abhorrence of war and perhaps violence, and could not in conscience fight in a war. **Others** just did not want to face death, and said they were not prepared to go. **Many of these** tried to find loopholes, and developed maladies that doctors said would save them from National Service. **There were a dozen other classes of arguments against conscription.**

With this war in particular, there were **many** objectors. In WWII, it was clear that this nation was under attack. **Not so in this case.** Many people, including the young men, had never heard of Vietnam, and had no worry about far-away China taking over Australia.

In May, the Government thought that it needed to toughen up the laws to stop the so-called **draft dodgers** avoiding their call to arms. It brought down a number of new regulations, and I will look at the major ones now.

Dob in a draft dodger. The military had realised that they had no list of who the young men were, so that many of them were simply not registering as they were required to do. So they now demanded that schools, universities, and employers give them the names that they needed. They also called on other citizens, including parents, to dob in any one who was dodging the draft.

Letters, Not a Red Fearer. My son has a legitimate reason to not register for the draft. But in a time of near hysteria, with people dobbing each other in, he can not be certain that he will not end up in the front line in Vietnam.

We have decided that we will move to a different State, that he will work for me, and join no clubs, churches, and apply for no licences. We will keep this up until this Vietnam madness is finished.

Letters, R Lewis. I am astounded and dismayed to learn that the Government is seeking the power **to throw into civil gaols** youths who refuse to comply with its National Service policy.

Is it really in the community's interest to force these young men who still have the time to become useful citizens to associate with, and even share cells with, criminal and depraved types in gaol?

Letters, E Mowbray. Some amendments aim at obtaining information from certain citizens, or groups of citizens, regarding the actions, or failure to act, of other citizens.

This is a reminder of the system of "informers" which has been one of the worst characteristics of Fascist and Communist countries. It is inconceivable that such legislation could be brought down in an Australian Parliament.

Letters, 10 Social Leaders. This patently unsatisfactory situation has prompted further legislation under which parents are to be compelled to supply information about their sons, and universities and other educational institutions to inform upon their students. These Government proposals introduce entirely new principles into Australian society - principles which we find subversive of the rights of the family and the duties of the teacher.

If there is to be such a thing as an issue requiring a free "conscience" vote in Parliament, **then this must be it**. To treat these grave matters as subjects for party political contest would be to inflict grievous injury upon our democratic institutions. There are divisions within the parties over these matters.

We therefore urge all members of Parliament to insist on voting according to their consciences - for the sake of conscience and in consideration of the moral issues which this Act and its proposed amendments have raised.

Letters, J Greenwood. Where an employer takes action to comply with Sec 55 and inform upon his employees, the effect upon employer-employee relationships may well be catastrophic.

The result could easily lead to resignations, or in larger concerns to go-slow tactics and strikes.

Any Act of Parliament imposing an obligation upon citizens to inform upon their fellows will undoubtedly be applied in other Acts as time goes on and particularly in Acts relating to taxation and company law.

Card burning. When the Military received a registration from a youth, it sent a response giving details of what would happen next. These draft cards were seen by some as the symbol of government compulsion, and so groups of recipients at times gathered together and lit a bonfire and burned their cards in a public display of defiance.

Letters, K Buckley. There is the new provision for a fine of $200 for destroying a draft card. This "crime" has nothing whatsoever to do with draft-dodging.

Card-burning is a gesture of defiance, a form of political protest. By subjecting it to this vicious penalty, the Government reveals its own uncertainty and fear of popular opposition. The action is on a par with the frequent attempts by Security to intimidate demonstrators by taking photographs of them.

There is still time for the Senate to eliminate this blatant infringement of civil liberties. The Government should be left in no doubt about one thing: card-burning will continue - principled young men are not so easily bullied - and if the Government dares to enforce this provision it will only make martyrs of those concerned.

Alternative forms of service. It was obvious that many youths who objected to going to war would be quite prepared to work in a peaceful way for the good of the nation.

The new regulations made no provision for this, and criticisms of this abounded.

Letters, Barry Tredinnick. We would have no problem in finding volunteers for National Service from our young people if they believed they were to be put to a task which had a purpose.

Let us form the Australian Civil Aid Group with a twofold purpose - helping within Australia and outside Australia.

AUSCAG should form a part of a new type of national service in which we could all have pride. AUSCAG could be truly aimed to enable our young people to be of service to our nation and our neighbours.

Letters, Horses for Courses. You can drive a horse to water but you can't make him drink. Suppose the Government makes a handful of young men go into the army, and prepares them for fighting.

I suggest that these young men will struggle against this every inch of the way, and be more trouble than they are worth. The effectiveness of an army unit depends on the unity and camaraderie between its members. There is no way that this can happen if a few members here and there are trying to buck the system.

There are many other posts for the non-belligerents,as medical orderlies, for example. Their oft-repeated offer to work in the desert to relieve this nation's shortage of water is one that should be accepted.

The Government should stop being a mindless bully, and intelligently accept the abundant resources offering.

Comment. The amendments to the drafting laws won no new friends. But they made a lot of enemies. **The delicate pendulum of public opinion got another nudge towards the "No to the war" side.**

A QUESTION FOR YOU

Suppose your 19-year-old son was a healthy outgoing lad, full of mischief and silliness, who was making the normal mistakes and yet working his way to responsible adulthood.

Suppose that, for some reason or other, he genuinely wanted to avoid all killing, and decided that he would not register with the authorities.

That would leave you in a difficult position. By law, the new law, you would be required to dob him in. The authorities would pursue him, and probably force him into military service and most likely send him off to Vietnam.

My first question is: Would you dob him in? If you did not, and the authorities found out, you would be hauled before a judge, and possibly a jury, your name would get into the papers, and there would be a few in society who would make sure that your name was mud.

What of your relationship with your son if you did? How would he respond immediately? What about in five years, Or 15 years. What if he was sent overseas, and what if he was killed?

These and other questions plagued parents now in 1968. Given the level of resistance to conscription, thousands of parents had to face up to them. What a dreadful decision to be forced into.

So, now I ask the question again. What would you do? Risk your son's life? Or do nothing, and face the opprobium of a breaker of the law?

PARENTS AND CITIZENS

Almost every school in the nation had a P and C Association. Their purpose was to give parents a say in the running of the school, and to raise funds for the school's facilities.

Initially, most schools had used their fund-raising activities to improve libraries and sporting facilities and the like. As time passed, some started **to donate money to causes that were far from home**. For example, at the moment a number of local units were combining to create a scholarship fund to provide higher school education for a few Aborigines.

The NSW Department of Education said this had now gone too far, and that funds raised by a local school must go towards the benefit of **that** school.

Quite a few people took exception to this.

Letters, M Michael, Rainbow Street P and C. Our Association is one of more 500 P and C Associations which have so far contributed more than \$7,000 to the Federation's Aboriginal Scholarship Fund. Scholarships have already been awarded to two Aboriginal students with good educational potential attending State High Schools, and the available funds are sufficient to assist several more capable Aboriginal students who would otherwise be forced by economic and social pressures to leave school at age 15.

Mr Cutler ignores the precedent of the Federation's recent Tasmanian Bushfire Appeal, to which we contributed generously without any objection.

Our Association strongly supports the declaration by the Federation President that the Federation would press on with the appeal despite the Minister's objection.

If the present rules do not allow P and C Associations to contribute to such public-spirited appeals through the Federation, then it is time the rules were changed.

Letters, B Backhouse. The Minister is quite agreeable to children attending Government schools contributing to the United Nations International Children's Emergency Fund. Whilst undoubtedly this is a very worthy fund, why this discrimination? Irrespective of which fund the contribution is being made to, it's the parents who pay.

Letters, R Wilkins. Nearly all associations pay affiliation fees to their Federation and to their district councils. **For a long time** a number of **these P and C councils have been sponsoring scholarships** with money contributed by the associations.

Affiliation fees are paid to youth organisations, cultural bodies such as the Australian Theatre for Young People and others. In the case of handicapped children's schools, their P and Cs pay membership fees to such organisations as the Australian Council for Mentally Retarded or other appropriate bodies. These links are not only desirable but necessary.

The Minister's veto on the Aborigines' Scholarship Fund has brought to a head the smouldering resentment of the P and C movement as the Department attempts to inhibit its activities.

Comment. The Minister for Education replied that such donations **would not be allowed in the future**.

However, there were some who thought that the Department had made a wise decision.

Letters, H Freeland. The rule disallowing P and C Associations supporting outside-of-school activities must remain.

It must be remembered that P and C moneys are held in trust for clearly specified uses and it is for these uses that I and some thousands of others devote our time and energy.

A parent or a citizen, however, should not be, and is not, deprived of the opportunity of supporting the Aborigines' Scholarship fund. The children of the High School with which I am associated organised a dance to raise money specifically for this fund and the parents who happened to be at the P and C meeting when the letter of appeal was read were happy to man the soft-drink and potato chip stalls, and to help in the proper conduct of the evening.

Mr Cutler, please do not alter the present rule!

Letters, It's our money. The P and C movement has lost its way. It started out trying to help children in their own schools with immediate need for better facilities. Now it had become the *Idle Mother's Movement*, where bunches of women try to do good for every capricious group their devious minds can think of.

The aim was, and still should be, to help our own children. When everything is perfect in our own schools, then the mothers should join **another** organisation and strive to further its aims. But never through the P and C movement.

SHARE PARCELS

There was a great share boom on all of Australia's stock markets. Mining stocks were very popular, and many a sober sensible household was having a bet. The problem for brokers was that these bets all of a sudden were becoming so small that brokerage paid to them did not cover the cost of servicing them.

So they decided that the minimum trade in low value shares should be raised to 100 shares. So that a punter who wanted to buy, and sell, a bundle of 10 shares might now have to buy 100. His costs, including brokerage, would make him hesitate, and clearly some would-be traders might have to think for a while before plunging.

Letters, D Lewis. For some time Australian Stock Exchanges have been fostering interest in the stock market by conducting education classes and encouraging small investors, so it is alarming to note the recent announcement to increase substantially the size of share parcels.

By limiting small investment, the Exchanges are stifling the interest of the beginner and small investor. Investors in Australia's development should not be restricted to wealthy citizens and organisations.

Letters, M Rickerby. It now means that a stock priced at 24 cents would cost $240 for a marketable parcel plus brokerage, as against $24 for a parcel at present plus minimum brokerage of $2.

The Government accepts amounts from as little as $20 on Special Bonds and the newly formed Resources

Development Bank accepts sums of $50, so why should the exchange require more?

Letters, M Benyon. If we are to retain a majority interest in our own future we must encourage more of the untapped capital lying idle in banks and appeal more to the great Australian gambling instinct to give share buying a go.

If we don't, there are plenty of overseas investors willing to take us over by our default - can we blame them?

Let the exchanges and the companies do their bit in the national interest by abandoning their proposals even if this means some increase in minimum brokerage and shaving of dividends.

Letters, Carey Smithers. In the past year, I have invested small amounts and have had good results but, under the new rule, I certainly would not be willing, or in a position, to wager a minimum of $250 as compared to $25-$50 on a so-called "tip."

I realise this is what they want, but how can one start out when once again the opportunities go to the man with plenty of money to spare?

Comment. The brokers were not deterred by the small loss of business threatened by these writers, and they stuck to the minimum parcel rules they had just announced.

It is only in recent times that these were relaxed. As computerisation occurred, brokers changed some of their minimum bundle rules, though they increased their minimum brokerage fee. So, in the long run, it still remains true that trading in very small lots is expensive. You would be better off at the TAB.

JUNE NEWS ITEMS

Major transplants, including the heart, have come to centre stage, so that **NSW and Victoria have suggested that doctors and hospitals stop doing them** until legal, ethical, moral and medical aspects of transplants have become clear....

Kidneys and corneas are excluded from the requests. **It is unlikely that doctors will accede to the request** because they already have a number of patients in hand. And because **doctors do not readily accept government intervention in medical decisions.**

June 6. **Senator Robert Kennedy was shot and killed in Los Angeles this morning.** He had just been very successful in the Californian Democratic primary election, and **was looking increasingly likely to win the Presidential race in a few months.** The killer was from the nation of Jordan, and initial speculation is that he was a Communist. In fact, he was not.

When the Queen's Birthday Honours were announced, **an Australian outsider surprised some. Zara Holt, was promoted to Dame.** She was **the widow of the late Prime Minister Harold Holt** who drowned six months ago while swimming in the surf.

Sometimes, **in the world of sports**, goodwill and sportsmanship prevail. But only sometimes. **In cricket** at the international level, **rivalry** between Australia and England **can be a little excessive. And in Rugby League**, it is even more robust and sometimes violent between these two same nations....

But it is when **Australia plays France in Rugby League** that **there is no enmity. Just pure hatred.** Every tour is the same. It starts with bonhomie, then degenerates into back-stabbing **off** the field and punch-ups **on** the field. **By the time the tour ends, open hatred prevails....**

This year, a special event was held, called **the World Cup.** The Aussies knocked out several other nations, and won the Final over France by a wide margin. A great feather in our cap, we were told....

No one told the French, apparently. At the Presentation after the game, they sat in the sheds and refused to come out. **Sulking.** The Australian crowd booed them liberally for this, but **secretly loved it. Sulking and hiding away.** What a fitting end to the tour!...

Sports between nations really do engender peace.

Sydney's Elizabethan Opera Company was due to stage the first night of a new season with a performance of *Tosca.* **The crowd arrived in gala gear, with furs, jewels, and splendid gowns and lots of glitter and glamour and champers.** Men also attended....

But it was all in vain. There was no opera. Half a dozen leading members of the cast were laid low with a flu, and could not raise a single warble. **The show did not go on.**

The UN General Assembly voted strongly in favour of a ban to stop the spread of nuclear weapons. France was one nation of the few that currently held the Bomb, but it **voted against the motion. More boos for France.**

HOME UNITS: NOT NEAR MY BLOCK

Home units had only been around the cities for a few years. Many Councils were toying with introducing areas for their construction, and a few actually had seen units constructed. But these were mainly on the fringes of suburbs, and restricted to two stories.

But the logic of these was inescapable to those who saw our cities growing, and our suburbs merging, and our cities becoming one united sprawl from one edge to the other. They claimed that the increase in population would be such that there would not be enough land to build our current cottages with big back-yards and the only way was to concentrate the population into multi-family units.

The opposition said that the growth of the cities should be stopped, backyards could be smaller, and some even suggested that family planning had its role. Further, some went on to say, if units **must** be built, ration them to small numbers, and keep them well away from existing suburbs.

This battle had been going on for a few years, and it came to a head in the conservative, old, sandstone suburb of Hunters Hill in Sydney. A meeting had been held, and 700 residents attended and demanded that progress should be eschewed, and in particular that further and bigger blocks of units were not welcome.

Arguments came to the newspapers from all directions. Some of them were just plain silly. For example, one person said that the average home unit housed one and a half people, and the average cottage housed five. Thus, she argued, houses were superior. I need hardly say that she overlooked the fact that eight units might be built on one site.

Other arguments were more logical. Higher density meant more rates, and thus more local amenities. If they were built near railway stations, less street parking would be needed. Some of the old houses were a shambles. They should be knocked down.

Letters, Gerard Draper. Thanks to the availability of better quality accommodation, people who were previously forced to live in sub-standard, cramped conditions have been able to move to unit-type accommodation in other suburbs.

The responses were immediate. It was a great loss to all if the leafy outlook of the older suburbs was replaced with bricks and tiles. Standing at the front fence talking over the rose garden would be come a thing of the past. Strangers would be walking the streets replacing the familiar faces of yesteryear.

Letters, G McGarry. Is there any reason why this type of development should spread like measles in spots all around nearly every station or wharf or other centre in this city?

Yet this is the type of thing which has been allowed happen over the last 10 years or so largely by default on the part of apathetic residents.

If people in all areas took action such as this or such as that taken by residents in Hunter's Hill, they may yet check the further spread of the great Australian ugliness in the form of poor and unsuitable development.

Comment. Only real die-hards seriously thought the epidemic of home units would be stopped or corralled to remote places. Already any one could see that units were starting to concentrate near railway stations and shopping centres. And soon enough, the continuous lines of 8-storey high units for the entire distance of city tracks would be obvious.

I agree on balance that the total amenity to citizens has been increased, and that we are better off than we were with the 1930's outlook. On the other hand, when I do find a pocket of that old world charm still unchanged, I get nostalgic for a while. But, I must admit, **only for a little while.**

PROSTITUTION

All of the cities in Australia had a thriving prostitution trade. Usually it centred in the heart of the city, in the older run-down suburbs. It was always the subject of complaints from residents and moralists, it was always being cracked down on by police, it was always the focus of crimes such as bashings and theft.

Sydney was no exception, and Chapel Lane, and its surrounds, could boast a flourishing trade that seemed never to have any seasonal downturns. That part of Darlinghurst, and neighbouring Woolloomooloo and Kings Cross, was under scrutiny as the city developed, and there was a lot of talk of grand plans for development of the wider area.

So, prostitution came under the microscope. But not, this time, for its vice and pimps, warts and pimples, but rather where it could go to if it was pushed to pastures greener. Also, what could be done with the area that was left behind. The tentative views expressed here do not reflect the views of the trade, which was quite determined that it would never move from its current gold-mine.

Letters C Wallace. The recently publicised sordid details of the vice activities in Chapel Street and Woods Lane adjacent to Woolloomooloo had been common and frustrating knowledge to the members of the City Council when administrating the affairs of this city.

Many attempts were made by the then City Council to deal with the problems which surrounded the residents in this area. These people, through mainly economic necessity, who were compelled to live on the periphery of this vicious, unhealthy centre of city life, were constantly complaining that the failure to eliminate these vice dens was not only causing them distress, but fear of violence when they voiced their protests against these nocturnal activities and sought council's assistance to eliminate this cesspool completely.

As a former alderman representing this area, I constantly advocated the demolition of these residences and the resumption by the council of the area for a full-scale multi-residential development where people could enjoy the benefits of living close to the heart of the city from whence they obtain their employment, and could bring their families up in an area with some confidence.

Surely this is now a golden opportunity for the Commissioners of the City of Sydney to proceed with such a scheme and eliminate for ever this blot on our city's life.

Failure to continue a scheme of residential development in Woolloomooloo to cater for the dispossessed families due to the Eastern Suburbs railway has aroused strong criticism and resentment, not only in the area but from the citizens generally. Here, Mr Treatt, is a chance, I believe, to justify your Commission in the eyes of the public.

Letters, Faith Fogarty. It is unrealistic of former Alderman C Wallace to think that eliminating the "cesspool" from the Chapel Street-Woolloomooloo areas would come anywhere near eradicating the blot of prostitution on our fair city. If prostitution were suppressed in one part of the city it would pop up in another without fail.

It would be too much to expect the Commissioners and councillors of Sydney and suburbs to take an enlightened approach to this ancient controversial problem, but if they do decide to face the facts they should observe what the Government in the city of Hamburg has done in an area off the Reeperbahn.

Realising that extermination of prostitution is impossible, they have removed the women from their old dwellings and put them in a large modern hotel-like building with regular health inspections, and, most important, have reduced the control of these women by racketeers, who constitute the really criminal and dangerous aspect of the business.

This letter is not meant as an apotheosis of prostitutes, but I do feel it is necessary that a realistic policy be devised to purge the business of its most disagreeable elements and try to control it rather than kick it from one spot to another.

Letters, C Wallace. My letter regarding the "cesspool" from the Chapel Street-Woods Lane area which Faith Fogarty has designated "unrealistic" is, on the contrary, an attempt to introduce realism into what appears to have become an emotional quasi-moral question.

Without canvassing her attitude, which appears to be one of condonation of prostitution, I believe that the vacated houses now untenanted and presumably owned by the RSPCA could be put to better use in this ideally situated area for residential purposes, and that a pursuance of the policy of the previous city council of providing high-density development of a residential nature in the city is nothing but a realistic and progressive step directed towards the betterment of the use of our space in the city.

If, as your correspondent believes, prostitution is an attitude which should be condoned by the Government, I agree with her it is not a question of a council to supervise the morals of a community, but on the question of location for such activities. It would seem to me that, based on newspaper reports of violent sex crimes and divorce proceedings emanating from the north side of the city, houses of ill-repute would find a more ready social acceptance there than in any area close or adjacent to the Woolloomooloo area.

Incidentally, the experiment by the Government in the city of Hamburg is in direct contradiction to that adopted by the Government of France, who found it necessary to abolish the legalised "maisons de joie" which had characterised the diminishing moral attitude of the French nation just subsequent to the last war.

OLD AND NEW THOUGHTS ON POLITICIANS

The *SMH* ran an Editorial which gave evidence that our elected representatives were far from perfect. This was a familiar refrain, that the following reader was happy to expound on.

Letters, Brian Sully. The harsh truth, of course, is that parliamentary government as we see it practised in this country has become in reality little more than a solemn form of mummery in which groups of generally mediocre machine politicians go through a series of motions which rarely result in more than a formal confirmation of the wishes of the executive Government.

This state of affairs is linked, of course, to the overall failure of all political parties to attract into public life men and women who do have imagination and initiative. The general rule is that existing preselection processes in the major political parties make it almost impossible for anyone to enter parliamentary public life who is not prepared to do some **pretty crude scheming** and compromising in order to "get the numbers" from among the usually very conservative groups who determine party endorsements.

We can only expect to find in Australia as in America that we have evolved into a predominantly urban society cramped into a social environment wholly incapable of meeting the needs and aspirations of its individual members. That such a situation is explosive can be seen in the recent social and political developments in America.

It is to be hoped that your timely editorial will stimulate an active public debate about the need for improved leadership in parliamentary government, and a resulting deliberate acceptance by people with proven qualities of real leadership of the need to become active politically, even within the daunting limits of the existing party structures.

If they don't, then the present leadership crisis - which is bad enough - will become a leadership vacuum, which will be immeasurably worse for all of us.

A few moments of self indulgence.

I have now almost completed 30 books in this series. Every now and then, I have indulged myself for a few pages, and got off the fence I normally sit on, and had my say. Nothing too violent, or bitter or even critical. Just a burst of youthful enthusiasm, coming from a mild person who has croissants for breakfast every Sunday.

So, I will indulge myself now by writing a few words on politicians.

Let me say at first that I do not expect too much from them as a group. After all, they are people just like all of us. We should not expect them to be better than we are, or even to have better judgement.

Add to this, the fact is that they **do** work hard in Canberra and **doubly hard** when they come home to their electorate. And further, they have to endure abuse and snide judgements from a large number of people, many of whom are too quick to criticise.

Having said that, I will voice just two of my pet political grouches.

The first one is a trivial matter, directed mainly at the leaders. **They should get out of the public eye.** Every night, they are on TV. Sometimes being cute in a classroom, sometimes walking through a shopping centre shaking hands. I would like to go back to Menzies, who gave a TV appearance once a week, and was prepared to save his wisdom for that occasion.

As I said, this is only a trivial matter. But from that, it becomes obvious that our politicians are driven, not by carefully thought-out policy issues, but rather by popular whimsy, by fear of the next poll, and the desire to score cheap points rehashing deeds and other people's failures of yesteryear.

So get them out of the limelight.

The second grouch is that I want them to develop proper policy. Some decent 5-year plans, that create or expand Australian industry. **For example**, they could set up, with private enterprise, industries that process our iron ore to the half-way stage, and then export it. Instead of just digging it out of the ground and selling it in its raw state. Think of the employment and value added.

If you do not like the iron ore example, substitute your own. But whatever you decide, I want the government to get off its backside and promote such schemes, instead of trying to balance the budget by robbing Peter and paying Paul.

That's it. The end of my self-indulgence. As usual, it may be that I look at it tomorrow and decide it is not fit to print, then you will see a two-page gap in this text where it would have been printed.

If it is in fact printed, please do not judge me too harshly. Simply put it down to the ravings of a writer who has spent 16 years writing 30 books, and is just getting a sniff of different pastures.

NEW IDEAS FOR OLD DISEASES

The Letter below brought a new idea for an old problem. In Australia, it was a novel idea at the time.

Letters, Confused Parent. I am the father of a 16-year-old boy who is a sufferer from epilepsy. His condition is under reasonable control, but he still experiences occasional fits.

These have mostly occurred when he is at home, but some months ago he became concerned that he might have a seizure away from home and that the nature of the seizure might not be recognised. He asked for a disc to wear on a chain around his neck, to carry the wording "I am an epileptic" on one side and his name and telephone number on the other.

This morning the situation arose and he had a seizure on a railway station. Several people came to his assistance, one of whom was a medical student. Apparently a thorough search was made of his wallet in case there was a card giving the required information, but his collar was not loosened and the disc was not discovered.

I have nothing but the highest praise and gratitude for the people who came to his assistance. But my concern here is that there is **no accepted form of identification for people who do have an affliction of this or a similar nature.**

Perhaps the medical profession can consider this problem and recommend a standard procedure which could be well publicised.

Comment. Here we have the start of a new mini-industry that **alerts various medical authorities to the patient's distress.**

QUICK QUOTES

Barry Humphries on where not to live:

"I hate the idea of living permanently in London, but the idea of living permanently in Melbourne is an equally appalling prospect."

Doctor Shirley Summerskill, British Labour MP, on women "changing from individuals to organised feminists in 1968":

"Problems arising from incomes policy will look like a cosy tea party compared with the chaos of a petticoat revolution."

JULY NEWS ITEMS

Six elderly women burned to death in a fire at Kew Mental Hospital in Melbourne's suburbia. **Hans Heysen,** well-known Australian landscape artist **died, aged 90.**

NSW and other States are talking about **giving 18-year-olds the right to vote.** It will be perhaps three years before such a measure could be put into place....

At the moment, **young men can be conscripted** and sent to Vietnam, and perhaps be killed, but they do not as yet have the vote.

The nation's first major toll road is being built. That will connect Newcastle and Sydney. But **it will take years for completion,** and is subject to the NSW Budget and strikes by the work force. Still, it is the first. **Possibly more will follow.**

Anti-war demonstrations are causing havoc in Sydney and Melbourne. Two in the last two days have each drawn over 2,000 protesters, mainly students and other young people. A popular venue for these demos is **outside the American Embassy**, and police are often injured. Mounted police help to control the mobs. 200 people were arrested in Sydney, amid the normal claims of police brutality.

In the world of Rugby League, three players were sent off in a Sydney First Grade match between South Sydney and Western Suburbs. One such player was **the popular Captain of Souths, John Sattler.** He said "a player spat in my face, so I spat back." League, as usual, was living up to its reputation.

CSIRO scientists have come up with a **plastic** coat to put on sheep to keep them warm in winter. **One million sheep die each winter in Australia** from cold and rain. The scientists are looking at alternatives to the plastic coat because **it might be too costly for most graziers.** They are trying throw-away water-resistant paper coats. **Hopefully they can be fitted and re-fitted easily between showers.**

A Sydney man, blind for seven years, has sent his **seeing-eye dog to a farm** at NSW's Tamworth. The dog has developed **a neurotic aversion to loud noises**, and must be moved to a quieter place....

"Three years ago, **a boy threw a fire cracker onto the dog's back.** It exploded there and since then he has become increasingly **sensitive to loud and sudden noises,** even a car door", said **the upset owner.** One consolation is that he will go to Melbourne this week to pick up a new dog.

A Committee of the **World Council of Churches** has made a remarkable call that **alters the basis for resistance to Vietnam call-ups....**

Previously, Churches would give support to objections based **only on religious grounds. In future,** they will support these, of course, but also others **not** based on religion. Matters **such as morals and ethics would now be considered....**

Little by little, the opponents to conscription are gaining ground.

THE SIEGE AT GLENFIELD

Glenfield was a small town on the sprawling outskirts of Sydney. A young man, a petty criminal called Wally Mellish, had just leased a house there, and was living with his girlfriend, aged 20 years. The girl, Beryl Muddle, had an infant son.

Police constables came to their front door to serve a summons for car theft. Mellish did not open the door, and instead fired a bullet over their heads. They soon returned to the scene with back-up that included the Riot Squad.

Mellish announced that he had a few guns and loads of ammunition on the premises. He also had a box of grenades. But importantly, he had two hostages, who he was threatening to kill if the police did not meet his demands.

Police procedures for hostage situations had not yet developed, so the NSW Commissioner of Police, Norm Allan, himself stepped in. He visited Mellish and started to bargain with him.

Mellish agreed to give himself up **if the Commissioner allowed him to marry the girlfriend**. This was arranged, the Commissioner and a Police Superintendent were witnesses, and **Allan paid for drinks and cakes to be brought in from a local shop. He also bought a 20 Pound ring for the groom to give to the bride.** Mellish had agreed to hand over his gun if the police left him alone for two hours after the ceremony.

But he reneged on this and set a new time limit of eight next morning. **This set the pattern for the next seven days.**

He would promise to come out, without the gun, if he got some concession, and then fail to live up to the promise. Over the period, Allan visited him regularly, and **Mellish even extracted an Armalite rifle and 200 rounds of ammunition from Allan**. The Armalite was reportedly used by crack-shots and snipers, and was said to be extremely accurate and powerful. **The Police Union thought this concession put their lives in danger. They were doubtless correct.**

The situation was made even more bizarre because Mellish used **fledgling talk-back radio** to tell the world his views of the world and his place in it, to a fascinated public. His new wife added her voice at times, and seemed to be comfortable and in no peril.

Listening to the radio, the police realised that they were in no danger of being shot, so they moved around and had barbeques and bonfires on the footpath outside the house. They also took shifts at night to throw rocks onto the tin roof of the house at 15 minute intervals, so that Mellish could not get a proper sleep.

After a total of eight days, Mellish surrendered. One last concession was that he be taken to an Army Recruitment Centre **to offer himself for military service in Vietnam**, "to make up for all the trouble he had caused." He was quickly rejected by the Army, and he was returned to Morisset Mental Hospital.

Two movies, were made of the episode, *Shotgun Wedding* in 1993 and *Mister Reliable* in 1996. Berryl Muddle left him soon after he surrendered. Mellish died in 2016.

Comment. Not everyone thought that the Commissioner had done a good job.

Letters, Mary Forbes. Commissioner Allan has been cavorting for days like an inept schoolboy at the beck and call of a deranged petty criminal.

I am not so distressed at Mr Allan failing to have the man effectively disarmed and the house cleared of weapons when he had the chance. But his part in obtaining a marriage licence at a few hours' notice was surely irresponsible. Marriage is a very solemn and serious business, and the law rightly stipulates a lapse of some weeks before a licence is granted, so that people cannot be rushed into matrimony on the spur of the moment.

And how much more important is that time for cooling off when the man is a deranged criminal and the woman is deemed too young and inexperienced to be allowed to vote!

Mr Allan not only allowed but actively encouraged the woman to take this tragic step. Who is Mr Allan that his honour as "a man of his word" should be zealously guarded at such a cost?

Hostage negotiation was in its infancy, so no one thought it strange for the Commissioner to take over. It is reported, here and there, that the Commissioner was particularly interested because he thought that Mellish was a small fry in a major car-stealing ring.

In any case, **the matter was settled without any loss of life**, and no harm done to any one. So, you could say that Allan's intervention worked. Though I suspect that modern-day negotiators might do things differently.

AN ASIDE ON VIETNAM

This siege was a simple local story, yet the passions of Vietnam were so pervasive that it was seen to provide a

moral salutatory lesson for the supporters of the Vietnam war.

Letters, W Dowe. The general disapproval of the Glenfield gunman, the great expense and lengths to which the community is prepared to go to save the woman and baby, are very encouraging. But they are in stark and strange contrast with the general apathy which we show towards the gunmen who with much deadlier guns and weapons slaughter and maim thousands of equally valuable women and children in Vietnam, and even honour those who perpetrate the horrors which are supposed to confer benefits on ourselves.

WHAT'S IN A NAME?

Abermain, as I suspect most of you know, in 1950 was the centre of the universe. At Christmas each year, my family would move from this coal-mining town and go to a place called *Arcadia* on beautiful Lake Macquarie. We would camp on the fore-shores there for the six weeks of the school holiday.

The only fly in this ointment was that **our re-directed mail** seldom got to us in a timely manner. This was because there was a suburb in Sydney also called *Arcadia*, and our mail-sorters gave **it** preference. Remember, there were no Post Codes back then.

To solve this problem, postal authorities suggested that **our** *Arcadia* be changed to something else. The local Post Master wanted *Kirkwood* for some personal reason, so he labeled his Post Office as such, and put up road signs on the inwards roads announcing that you were now entering

Kirkwood. Somehow, the vox populi was heard after a while, and the township was called *Arcadia Vale.*

But the whole process took five years, and during that time many letters were late or lost or destroyed, and many a temper was frayed.

Situations such as this were common. Suburbs and towns were free to bandy around names for themselves and their streets, lanes, knolls, streams more or less at will, with no centralised control

In 1966 NSW, in common with other States, established **the Geographical Names Board.** By 1968, it reported that 6,000 place names were assigned over the last year. Priority was given to perpetuating the names of deceased eminent persons, especially those of explorers. Also, euphonious Aboriginal names were looked upon kindly.

This report stimulated a wave of response. I have picked out those that deal with **Aboriginal names.**

Letters, Jean Edgecombe. I notice with interest a letter, "All in the name", wherein the Secretary of the Geographical Names Board states, among other things, that it is the board's policy to assign euphonious Aboriginal words as place-names under the Act to new areas.

How does the Board then reconcile its current proposal to assign the name "Westleigh" to a new suburb west of Thornleigh, especially when euphonious Aboriginal names have been suggested as alternatives?

Four names, Daneena, Nanbaree, Kurleah and Daringar, were suggested to Hornsby Council by the Board itself, and Elouera Park by a number of Thornleigh residents in a petition to Council. The latter name is significant in view of the fact that the new suburb is bounded on the west and south by Elouera Bushland Natural Park.

"Westleigh" has no meaning, except as a corruption of West Thornleigh, it has no historical significance and will be no easier to spell than an Aboriginal name. The Board will accept objections to this name, and suggestions, until July 14.

Letters (Rev) G Watts. The current discussion of Aboriginal place-names leads me to renew a suggestion which I made some years ago - that the Northern Territory be given the distinctive and beautiful name of Ananda, after one of the largest groups of Aboriginal tribes. At the time when my suggestion was first made, it was proposed in certain quarters to call the Territory "Kingsland"! How vile!

Letters, W Tucker. Rev Collocott is echoing the thoughts of a former redoubtable cleric, John Dunmore Lang who, in his earlier attack on anaemic place names, gave us a potpourri of Aboriginal nomenclature reading:

I like the native names as Parramatta,

And Illawarra, and Woolloomooloo;

Nandowra, Woogarora, Bulkomatta,

Tomah, Toongabbie, Mittagong, Meroo;

Buckobble, Cumleroy and Coolangatta,

The Warragumby, Bargo, Burradoo;

Cookbundoon, Carrabaiga, Wingecarribbee,

The Wollondilly,Urumbon, Bungarribee.

We all like them, but who can pronounce these interesting native names?

"Cadibarrawirracanna," which belongs to a lake near Coober Pedy, is one of the longest Aboriginal words, meaning "beautiful waters under the stars." From the tongue of the Aboriginal it is a delightfully sounding name. I can only see "Canna" in it for the commuter.

Letters, R Lowndes, Toongabbee. Your correspondent W Tucker, referring to Aboriginal place-names, prompts me to write in regard to the contemporary spelling of these names, as compared to the early original manner.

His letter referred to Toongabbie among many others, some of which correctly had the last syllable as "bee", whereas Toongabbie was given, and is, spelt with a "bie."

As early maps and documents refer to its spelling as Toogabbee, why has it together with other Aboriginal names been altered?

Now, in the great tradition of the theatre, I have saved the best till last.

Letters, J Edgar. It was interesting to read Mr W Tucker's translation of the Aboriginal word "Cadibarrawirracanna."

No doubt meanings are associated with the words in John Dunmore Lang's potpourri. To that collection may be added Wallangarra, Woodenbong, Ginnabri, Giligulgul and many others.

However, some 30 years ago the late Rev John Flynn of the Australian Inland Mission, in one of his earliest publications of the "Inlander", drew attention to a native settlement in the Norther Territory entitled Warrawarrapiraliliullamalulacoupalunya.

Borrowing Mr Tucker's descriptive terminology, the aforementioned location "from the toungue of the Aboriginal would also be delightfully mellifluous."

But what is its interpretation?

Comment. My wife types all my Letters for these books. I had to promise her time and a half for these last few.

BLACK POWER IN OZ?

The US was still unsettled by the murders of Martin Luther King and Robert Kennedy. Riots in US Southern cities and on University campuses were common, and black orators were stirring emotions across the nation. Australia had remained almost immune from this activity, but the *SMH* thought it sensible to have a look at the status of blacks in Australia.

A journalist reported in the Saturday's Features page. He chose a 19-year-old Aboriginal living in a tough inner-city suburb of Sydney who was likely to have had a particularly hard time. And indeed, the lad **had** been given a hard time. He chronicled earlier family neglect, several bashings by whites, and some hospitalisations, verbal abuse, and serious attacks on his dignity as a person.

Comment. It made sad reading. But if it was meant to stir readers into great indignation, it did not. **It was too late.**

Australian society was already aware of the injustices that were handed out to lads like him. For the last decade, most responsible people and groups had been gradually realising that they had a responsibility to improve the lot of the Aborigines, and had been doing what they could to fix things. Even the Governments, all of them, had been passing laws and regulations that brought incremental relief. In fact, in the next year, the Federal Government would hold a referendum proposing to give the vote to Aboriginals. This passed with over 90 per cent of the population approving in all States.

What I am saying is that society had moved a long way in the last decade, and the tough stories from the *SMH* article were well known. And, in a haphazard, almost random manner, most individual Australians were prepared to act to make recompense.

RESPONSE TO THE ARTICLE

Having said that, I enclose below a sample of the Letters stirred up by the article.

Letters, Margaret Tuckson. I wish every white person in Australia could read the interview "This is what it's like to be black" by Christopher Sweeney and feel shame for their race to the bottom of their boots.

This interview should be reprinted as soon and as often as possible.

Letters, Charles Huxtable. David Armstrong, the half-caste Aboriginal interviewed by Christopher Sweeney, should take the wise step of coming on side with decent white people who hate white gangsters and bullies as much as he does.

He was not attacked because of his colour. He was attacked because the white barbarians who roam our city streets will attack anyone who is weaker in size or in numbers. Unfortunately it happens daily in every city and town. A victim does not have to be black.

I am somewhat critical of David Armstrong's complaints. For instance, why should he live in a four-bedroom house with 26 others? He is a labourer in Port Kembla. He can certainly afford a better standard of living than that for himself.

Let me offer one practical suggestion towards raising the standard of dignity and welfare of young Aboriginal men. Let the Federal Government form an Aboriginal battalion of the Royal Australian Regiment for home defence. It would be difficult to devise any more speedy or practical method of uplifting the self-respect and material welfare of young Aboriginal men or of increasing public esteem for their manliness and efficiency. To see them march through our city streets would be an inspiration to many, and a stimulus to others who need it.

Comment. Charles Perkins was our first Aboriginal University graduate. Though he expressed his opinions readily, he was a moderate and thoughtful leader of the cause.

Letters, W Barker. Poor Charles Perkins! When he spoke about "black power" in Australia few did him the courtesy of reading below the headlines. What he said was that Aborigines have the capacity to wield a certain amount of power in the community and that to alleviate their problems they should use this power to prod the Government into activity. The methods Mr Perkins outlined fall into four groups: Political, economic, social pressure, violence.

Violence was mentioned by Mr Perkins as a possibility, but was not advocated by him. In his own words **"violence can be avoided and is certainly only the last resort. The Aboriginal people can only lose if they accept this alternative."**

Recent imputations that Mr Perkins is something of a rabble-rouser have done a grave injustice to a man who has made a sensitive and intelligent appraisal of the plight of the Australian Aboriginal.

Letters, Ann Brooks. For a number of years I have been reading of the constant clashes between black man and white, and I just had to have my say about this so-called "black power."

First, I am an Aboriginal and proud of it. During my working years, when I laboured side by side with white people, I have come to place them in three groups:

(1) The white man who considers the black to be dirt beneath his feet and to be treated as such. This white man in nought. He's nothing. He means as little to me as I to him and he's not much use to himself, much less the Aboriginal.

(2) The white who works with Aboriginals and shows no sign of "colour" outside his own private world. He and the Aboriginal will toil happily alongside each other day by day and share many hours of comradeship, but **this white man won't invite the Aboriginal to his home**. He can't mix with them after working hours and sometimes won't even so much as nod should you come across him in company.

(3) The white man who accepts the Aboriginal as he finds him and who sees no difference in any man. This white man has my deepest respect at all times and we of the coloured race love him. Without him we'd fail every time, because he helps us when we're down and gives us the encouragement which we so often need, time and time again.

Mr Charles Perkins, who has claimed that "black power" could occur in Australia, could not have met many of the white people from Group 3. He would never have made such a stupid remark if he had. If you think, Mr Perkins, for one minute that I can picture my friends or family racing around with machineguns tucked under their arms and home-made bombs strapped to their sides, waiting for a foolish white man to poke his nose out, then sir, you're out of your mind!

Sure we want better conditions, sure we want equal rights, sure we want a better deal. But we won't get them by "black power," nor will it be got by sitting on our behinds and moaning about it.

If we don't get off our backside and steadily but surely begin to better our own standards, how the hell is anyone else going to help us?

There is no value to any single thing if it hasn't been worked for, and no sense in trying to help those who won't be helped.

Comment. The black power movement in America continued on for years. In fact, there are still vestiges of it not far beneath the surface even today. But in Australia, the more conciliatory attitude of the average white Australian helped avoid the riotous events of the USA. Importantly too, the non-combative character of the Aborigines helped here too.

QUICK QUOTES

Victor Jury, film star bad guy, on his career:

"I have killed more old ladies, kicked more babies, kicked more people off the kerb, and strangled more canaries than anyone else in the world. But I always come to a bad end."

Sir Alister McMullen, President of the Senate, on an overseas Parliamentary tour:

"It will be no jaunt. We will be working hard."

Dr R Dowling, Senior Lecturer of Philosophy, University of NSW:

"I would say that 25 per cent of undergraduates are not worth having here. At least 15 per cent are academic rubbish. They are charming people, but not worth wasting time on."

AUGUST NEWS ITEMS

Over the last decade, the Roman Catholic Church has **debated many of its long-standing dogmas**, and has made superficial changes to some. As an aftermath to this, the Catholic world has been waiting for Pope Paul II's decision on **whether they can use artificial methods of birth control. That is, in this case, the Pill....**

He had decided that they can't. This decision **disappointed vast numbers of the faithful**, and would gradually promote further the **lessening of the influence of religion** right round the world.

The **number of migrants** coming to Australia last year was 137,000. But 23,000, from previous years, **returned to their homeland**. Most of those returning were British, who got homesick for the British weather....

Apart from that, it seems that many **British** had come on assisted passages, **on a trial basis.** "We will see how it works out". **Europeans were more determined** to stick it out, with most of them determined to make **a new start in life in a new country**.

The number of **US Servicemen visiting Australia on R and R** would rise **to 7,500 a month** by November. **Most will go to Sydney.** Only one in 100 go to the country or the Gold Coast.

The **NSW Minister for Education** was cornered by students demonstrating for more pay as he entered the Town Hall. **They tried to take his trousers off**, but the Police came to his rescue....

He said "I was assaulted by some **girls** as I entered the Hall. At least I thought **they were girls because they were all long-haired**"....

This **cutting** remark was a reference to **the fashion** of some young men to have long lank, and reputedly dirty, **long hair.** **"Long-haired gits" was the term of endearment** for the young men so afflicted.

Richard Nixon has been chosen as the 1968 Republican **candidate for the Presidency.** He beat Ronald Reagan in the Primary. This is **his second attempt** to win that office. In 1960 he was beaten by John Kennedy.

Wally Mellish has been rushed to hospital for X-rays because he has probably **swallowed open safety pins** while in Morisset Mental Hospital.

In London, at a meeting of 460 **Anglican and Episcopal Church leaders,** the proposition was discussed that women should be welcomed as priests and even bishops. This was the **first major congress** where the issue was raised.

The Federal Government has given approval for **Mary Kathleen Mines to sell 5,000 tons of uranium oxide ore to Japan. Of course, such sales in 2017 are not allowed** under Government policy.

The **food-freezer industry** activities are being called scandalous. They involved cutting up the carcase of a steer, say, and selling it **and the freezer** for home freezing. Reports are that the quality is bad, the carcases are not preserved, and that the carcase is all bones and the freezers break easily.

POPULATE AND GO TO HEAVEN

Pope Paul II disappointed half the Catholic world when he refused women permission to use the Pill as a contraceptive device. Back in 1961, Pope John XXIII started a series of Councils of Catholic Bishops, called Vatican II. This ambitious programme lasted until 1965, and talked a lot about liberalisation of the Church's dogma, and reforms of its processes and liturgy. In fact, it did not achieve much.

For example, it allowed the Mass to be said in English, instead of Latin. It allowed kids strumming banjos to partake in a few services. It allowed some clergy, at certain times, to parade in civilian clothes. But all the major stuff remained unchanged. For example, 2,000 years of the theological basis of Catholicity were not challenged. The Church hierarchy in Rome and round the world still manipulated the masses and their priests and monks and nuns. No semblance of democracy or criticism was brooked, and any form of questioning was likely produce a summons to talk things over in Rome.

When the four Councils were over, though, hope remained that a new Pope would reverse probably the most unpopular ruling it had maintained. That was, it was hoped that Paul II would approve the use of the Pill for Catholic couples.

But he did not. After a long delay, he said that Catholics must limit the size of their family **only by abstaining from sexual activity during fertile periods**. That was, no sex for one week a month, to be safe.

This placed millions and millions of families around the world in an impossible situation. Both mother and father were practising Catholics, going to Church at least on

Sundays, and taking Communion. They were now told that unless they heeded the Pope, they were no longer welcome. Not only that, if they then died, they would go directly to Hell.

Half the clergy in the world were equally distressed. **Some of them stalled**, and told their flocks that, **in this matter, the Pope did not speak for God**. No one swallowed that because for 100 years the Church had taught that the Pope was infallible when he spoke on matters of faith or morals.

Other clergy defended the edict. They said it was not important what individual people wanted. **The Church was not a democracy.** The popular vote did not count. Could a Church be respected if it changed its doctrines every time there was a swing in popular culture?

So, the battle raged on in the newspapers. The arguments, for and against the Pope, were ingenious, but mainly the same as the ones above. Often they spruiked the Bible, or famous philosophers. One camp argued that **the population of the world would continue to increase** and Africans, South Americans, and Biafrans would continue **to starve to death**.

The other camp stressed God's will, and offered quotes from the Bible to show what he wanted. One reader said that **in Australia using the Pill should be a sin**, because our natural birth rate was so low. **In India, it should be welcomed.** Another writer talked about "**sterilising Indians and Chinese** as if it were a matter of sterilising fruit-flies."

Another gave the pithy opinion; "Ban the Pill: Man's inhumanity to woman." I am not sure what she meant, but it's a good slogan to use if logic deserts you. A doctor said he was a Catholic, and he believed if he consented to a woman taking the Pill, he would be guilty of a mortal sin. So he would not do so.

The Papers were deluged with Letters. Some of them were sensible, and even more showed ignorance or bigotry or both. Because of space requirements, I can give you only three such. You can work out for yourself which class they fall into.

Letters, Lorraine Jackson. All through the ages, mass crimes have been committed in the name of religion, but this ruling by the Pope could surely be the most criminal and far-reaching of all.

This little man in his ivory tower has raised his hands, not to bless on this occasion, but to curse the millions as yet unborn who will slowly die from starvation. This is not probability or maybe, but fact confirmed over and over again.

Is it any wonder that we turn **from** the domination of Churches and retarded religions **to** commonsense ethics which allow men the right to live, and sanction the acceptance of scientific advances which allow them the right to live adequately?

Letters, Noel Lindblom. The dismay of your editorial on the Pope's decision to maintain the birth-control ban on the grounds that it sets the Church "against the realities and demands of modern life" is understandable but hardly logical.

As I understand it, the debate on birth-control within the Church was concerned with a conflict between this reality and the **perennial reality of the Church's central tradition**. The Pope, holding to the central tradition, was right to hand down his harsh judgment and he would be right to hold it in the face of mass defection of members, in the teeth of the "population explosion," and despite all appeals to humanism and commonsense.

The very phrasing of your editorial - "the Pope's ruling must appear as a disastrous miscalculation" - shows how far we have slipped. As if a great religious leader should shuffle with beliefs and timings like a politician! Like you, I have goodwill for the Church and would wish it to pursue its mission for good. But "prosper"? If the Pope's encyclical leaves him Pontiff of a handful of true Christians, it will have achieved a great mission for good.

Letters, Michelle Cronin. As the Catholic mother of two little children, I hurried to ask a priest today to explain the meaning of the Pope's statement. He failed to satisfy me, but assured me that "distinguished theologians" could. So could I use your columns to ask the distinguished theologians, whoever and wherever they are, to explain how any statement can be "one step removed" from being infallible (Bishop Muldoon's words). **To me that sounds like being one step removed from being pregnant.** As any woman knows, that is very, very different from being pregnant.

The issue persisted in the Press for as long as any other this year. But to **no avail for the "sinners."** The Pope was not swayed by the outcry from half a billion of his constituents, and kept the ban in place.

It still remains, sometimes **with the same equivocation,** throughout the world today.

POLL FINDINGS

Readers of this book will be doing so fifty and more years after 1968. They will have seen polls in the US for the election of President Trump, and polls for the British vote on Brexit. In both cases, these polls were horribly wrong.

This 1968 Letter below suggest that there is nothing all that new in this.

Letters, Geoff Hasler. It should be made clear that poll findings are by no means correct. They have made some superb miscalculations, e.g. in the 1948 Presidential elections in the United States. Every public opinion survey forecast a victory for Thomas Dewey over President Truman. Walter Lippmann accused Truman of "stubborn pride" for asking the Democratic convention to nominate him. In the event, Truman swept back into power, carried 28 States and had an amazing margin of 114 electoral votes.

At home, polls on the eve of the 1967 Senate elections predicted a strong swing to the Government; we all know that result.

LITTER AT GLENFIELD

In the aftermath of the Glenfield siege, this Letter asks everyone to be more tidy next time.

Letters, Gwen Simpson. Why is it that Australians can never congregate without making their meeting place a garbage dump?

In Wednesday night's television review of the Glenfield siege, viewers were shown the disgusting array of rubbish that has been dropped in Glenfield Road during the past week - beer bottles, cans, cartons, food wrappings, fruit peels, etc., etc.

This litter has been left by two sections of the community from which we might expect rather better behaviour - the police whose conduct is supposed to be exemplary, and newspaper men, many of whom have undoubtedly written articles on "filthy Sydney."

Viewers also saw a camp fire which has been burning continuously for seven days. Would it be so difficult to throw rubbish on to the fire rather than to scatter it indiscriminately? The commentator mentioned that the men waiting for developments were bored and frustrated; perhaps it would ease their boredom if they occupied the time clearing up the garbage they themselves scattered.

A LETTER ABOUT VIETNAM

I include a Letter from a supporter of the Vietnam war. At the moment, I am avoiding mention of the place as much as possible, because if I tried to report it properly, I would have no space for anything else.

But I simply can't let this Letter pass unacknowledged. It is so full of hatred and vitriol that it cries out for a place in this little History of mine. It has no vestige of fact or logic, it is pure abuse. I hope you enjoy it as much as I do

Letters, Will Brandt. I am disgusted and indeed alarmed at the cheap, low-brow publicity and sympathy in some quarters given by the Press, radio, and TV to draft-dodgers, cowards, anti-Vietnam, and in fact anti-everything students.

These long-haired, bearded, Godless oafs, with their "anything goes society," have been completely brainwashed by the red professors and teachers who have been allowed to infiltrate our schools and universities.

These social misfits who defy any sense of law and order, who have never heard of the word discipline, are in their insidious way endeavouring to undermine the whole concept of decent, respectful living, and their aims are to destroy all Western culture to make way for the **Hitler-minded rulers in the Kremlin**.

BULL-FIGHTING ANYONE?

The *SMH* ran a feature article that described a journalist's encounter with bull fighting in Spain. The article was inspired by an incident at a recent fight in Madrid. Spain's most famous matador, with a ton of pomp and two tons of flashy clothing and trumpets, was about to finish off a by-now helpless bull. Unexpectedly, "a rival matador entered the ring in street clothes. He strolled up to the bull, kissed it, stroked its horns, leaned casually on its forehead, and waltzed the half-ton animal round the ring. He exclaimed for all to hear that this was not a bull, it is a lamb."

The rival was fined for his intervention. A week later, when the rival was fighting, a supporter of the original matador ran into the ring, and pulled the bull by the tail, and it hardly reacted it was so docile.

Now all Spain, according to the report, is asking whether the matadors are fooling the public by pretending to take risks against tame animals.

Back here is Oz, defenders and opponents of the sport jumped into the ring.

Letters, A Craston. I am writing in defence of the bullfight. Tim Dare's primary objection appears to be that the bullfight is not an equal contest. He has missed the point.

The bullfight is not to be judged by Anglo-Saxon standards of sportsmanship. Man's struggle against death is not a game played according to some school-boy conventions, it is an unrelenting, unfair and losing struggle. Man always dies - in the bullfight the bull dies. The bullfight, to quote Ernest Hemingway, "is a tragedy not a sport, and the bull is certain to be killed."

I recommend Mr Dare to read Hemingway's "Death in the Afternoon," Angus McNabb's "Bulls of Iberia" and "To the Bullfight Again," by John Marks. If he is still interested he should select a fine Spanish Sunday afternoon and watch someone of the stature of Antonio Ordonez or El Viti in the Plaza. Then, perhaps he, too, will experience the bitter-sweet emotion that only the bullfight can produce.

Letters, T Atkinson. A Craston feels a "bitter-sweet emotion" at the sight of a bull fighting, without any chance at all of winning, and dying on a fine Sunday afternoon. Was the fineness of the day necessary? On other Sunday afternoons, fine or not, others have sallied forth on days long and happily gone by to throw missiles at poor slobbering lunatics chained in the confines of Bedlam, or to watch a bull being cruelly baited with a long sharp fork, or a bear forced to dance on hot bricks. Or, to go further back, to watch human beings being slowly and hideously tortured to death, and protesting if the process was not likely to last the whole long fine Sunday afternoon.

Only an inbuilt sadism was necessary in those days, so different of course from Hemingway's bitter-sweet emotions.

Happily this bitter-sweet emotion is coming under a cloud in these enlightened days, and those who delight in it are becoming fewer. Even in Spain itself the more healthy minded throng to the Soccer fields and leave the bullfighting arenas to the brash, impressionable tourist.

May it not be long before even these become enlightened and enable the world to get on with good clean living.

Letters, Laurence Benton. I have read "Death in the Afternoon" and "Bulls of Iberia," mentioned by Mr Craston. They made me sick. If there is anything almost as nauseating as bullfighting, it is the phony mystique with which its followers surround it - "moment of truth," "a tragedy, not a sport" - and all the rest of such meaningless claptrap.

Comment. Some thirty years ago in Australia, several entrepreneurs canvassed public opinion preparatory to starting bull-fighting here. They could make a strong economic case for doing that, and their claims that it would attract large numbers of tourists from Asia were seductive. Also, it seemed likely that all sorts of local industries would be born and flourish, with benefits for all.

Arguments against it came from the **animal welfare groups**. But the main opposition came from **the average Australian individual** who just thought this type of cruelty was going too far. They could accept that a good steak on a plate in the evenings was within the pail, but to deliberately set out to painfully weaken, and then kill, such magnificent beasts was going too far.

That is why you have to find something else to do on sunny Sunday afternoons.

FINAL WORD ON THE PILL

At the end of the month, Letters were still being published on the Pope's decision. I add here one final Letter on the matter, not to say that "here is the winning Letter", rather to emphasise the point that the moral dilemmas and the consequences and the torments for practising Catholics were real, huge, and **on-going**.

Letters, A Sparkes. I wish to associate myself with the general tenor (though not necessarily with all the statements) of the letter signed by Mr and Mrs Nelson and eleven other of my fellow-Catholics.

There appear to me to be so many plain errors of fact in or presupposed by the Pope's encyclical that its conclusion cannot be accepted as a statement of the divine law or as absolutely binding in conscience.

This would be an analogy: Suppose the Pope issued an encyclical forbidding the eating of pineapples on the ground that pineapples were dangerously hallucinogenic and turned their eaters into murderous monsters. Respect for the Pope's position would lead me to regard the prohibition as legally valid. The preposterousness of the reasoning behind it would lead me to the conclusion that the Pope was ignorant of the relevant facts about pineapples and that, therefore, the prohibition would not bind in conscience. In other words, when there were good reasons for eating pineapples, one could do so regardless of the prohibition.

It seems to me, therefore, that there are cases and circumstances in which the practice of contraception is not only morally licit but morally obligatory.

QUICK QUOTES

Arthur Calwell, Leader of the Opposition until 1967, aged 72:

"I would rather trust the young for all their mistakes than people of age 50, 60, and 70 whose minds have been fossilised."

London Daily Telegraph, on a report that West Indian Immigrants had eaten their landlord:

"Cases of suspected cannibalism can hardly fail to exacerbate local tension."

SEPTEMBER NEWS ITEMS

For cricket followers. **Gary Sobers** is currently touring Britain as **Captain of the West Indies team**. He set a record by **hitting a six off every ball of a six-ball over** at Swansea. The bowler said "if we still had eight-ball overs I would have got him. **I was just about to spring a trap.**"

A man standing on the crowded platform at Sydney's Central Station **leaned forward as he went to sneeze**. This **propelled his head** into the path of an approaching train, which **hit him on the temple**. He was taken to hospital, and is in a critical condition.

The Olympic torch was in Madrid. As it was passed from one runner to another, **it blew up due to a gas mishap**. It was re-lit by one of the three spares, and is now on a sloop taking it to the Canary Islands and then to **the 1968 Olympic venue in Mexico City**.

Biafra was a State of Nigeria. From 1967, its Igbo population **moved to secede**. The Nigerian Government and Biafra **entered into a civil war** and, as part of this, **Biafra was blockaded** and imports confiscated by the Nigerians....

Pictures of dying Biafran children flooded the world, and relief agencies were sending aid. Much of this was caught by the blockade....

From **1968 to 1970, well over one million Biafran children died of starvation**.

43 **hair-pieces, or wigs, were stolen** from one hairdresser in Sydney. They turned up later in the day in the displays

of another hairdresser. This second person has been charged with **receiving stolen goods**.

The **MCC** is the body that controls **the overseas tours** that the English Cricket Team makes. It has decided that **a coloured man**, Basil D'Oliveira, now playing legitimately in England, **should be excluded from the MCC tour of South Africa....**

Coloured cricketers in South Africa are not selected for the national team, and the Brits are accused of **caving in to pressure from the white supremacists in that nation.** Eleven members of the prestigious MCC have resigned, and over a thousand letters of protest have been received from its very British membership....

D'Oliveira now will be reporting on the Test series for a British newspaper. It remains to be seen whether he will get **special exemption from the South Africa's laws and be admitted to the white Press Box.**

A reminder of a forgotten world: "Roughrider Raymond Blades is in hospital with **a broken leg** sustained while breaking the **bulldogging record at Gurley rodeo.** Blades was injured in the last few minutes of a two-day fixture which netted a gate of more than $1,000."

The Federal Government **will promote sailing ships from around the world** visiting Australia late next year to **celebrate Captain Cook's so-called discovery of Australia in 1770.** One feature will be **a race from England to Australia.** It is hoped that the magnificent Chilian *Esmeralda* will attend.

WORLD TROUBLE SPOTS

There were plenty of places to worry about, other than Vietnam. **Czechoslovakia** was one of **a dozen nations** that Russia had controlled since the war. **This ring of nations** now provided a shield for Russia against attack from its west, and if any serious attempt was made to interfere with its hegemony, it put its foot down briefly, but in no uncertain manner, and squashed anyone in the way.

The Czechs had recently tried to do their own thing, and Russia then had used its customary violence to let them know who remained as master. Many nations protested loudly, and the UN condemned Russia. But to no avail, since Russia could veto any action against it, and many of the Red nations supported it anyway.

In Nigeria, the State of Biafra wanted to leave the Federation. They rose in revolt against the central Government and as a result, Biafrans were being starved and killed, and the Nigerians were seen as the oppressors. It was not all clear cut, since **Biafra was trying to secede**, and the Nigerians could say they were illegally attempting to do this by force, and had to be resisted by whatever means were available. Many nations opposed the Nigerian actions, but again the big nations were split, with France and others finding merit in the Nigerian argument.

In **South Africa**, apartheid was keeping the blacks and whites separated, with the whites holding all the cards. Criticism abounded from **the world's nations**, but many of **them** were in **the same boat**.

In **Rhodesia**, the white Smith Government had taken control and proclaimed that it was now independent of

Britain. That meant that a quarter of a million whites would dominate tens of millions of blacks. The UN had called for trade sanctions and the cutting of sporting ties with Rhodesia. Australia had done both of these.

In short, there were trouble spots all over the world, but there was **no unanimity at all** about who was in the right, and what to do about these situations.

One remedy was to use **economic sanctions** against a nation. But this never worked, because the sinning nation could always find someone else who was happy to supply them or take their produce.

Sporting sanctions were just plain silly. First of all, they were only applied by one sporting body against another. For example, Australia could refuse to play cricket or Rugby Union against South Africa. But in the scheme of things, apart from the tut-tut implied, what effect would they have? Secondly, a few games of sport here and there have no economic consequences worth mentioning.

The same applies to banning Rhodesia from the 1968 Olympics. This is a trifling matter that will affect only a few families, and will be not make any sort of dent on the nation's fortunes. Talk of such bans was common at the time, but the talk and the bans helped nothing.

So, the world was watching many events unfold, but **could find no way of bettering the lot of most sufferers**.

I will illustrate this with a closer, but brief, look at the situation in Biafra.

All correspondents here agreed that "the continuation of hostilities, the delay of food and medical relief, and the retribution of the Nigerian Federal Forces will contribute to the most blatant act of genocide since Tibet and on a scale of misery unequalled in the postwar world."

All agreed that "the Australian Government should strive for an immediate cessation of hostilities, urge restraint on a vindictive Nigerian Federal Government, and assist in reducing the delay of emergency relief to the Biafran people." And most sympathised with the idea that the Australian Government should co-ordinate the work of relief and charitable agencies.

Others went further.

Letters, Garth Nettheim. The world will **recognise the independence of Biafra** and give it all the aid that is required to preserve its independence from a regime which shows such callous disregard for innocent people. Whatever the rights and wrongs which produced the conflict, the cause of Biafran secession has acquired substantial justification from the ruthlessness employed to suppress it.

Our Government should do **something**. It could even take a lead in some way. To say and do nothing only compounds the sorry spectacle of man's inhumanity to man by a demonstration of man's indifference to man.

Most of the writers went on to further criticise the Australian Government for its inactivity.

Letters, David Nelson. The silence of our Government in the face of the Biafran tragedy is a national disgrace. One feels that our Government is more concerned with protocol governing relations between members of the Commonwealth than the wholesale murder of children and the deliberate extermination of an entire race now apparently in progress in Biafra.

There has not been the slightest hint that our Government has made any representations to **stop**

English arms being supplied to the Nigerian Government

Letters, Richard Ackland. It seems strange that **the United Nations**, which was so quick to condemn the actions of the Rhodesian Government by imposing economic sanctions, is so reticent to do the same to the Nigerian Federal Government. Any injustice or losses of human dignity that the Smith regime may have perpetuated appear quite paltry, in comparison to the Nigerian Government's deliberate annihilation of one of Africa's most intelligent and able tribal people.

It is a great tragedy that **the Australian Government** has not grabbed the opportunity to improve its rather odious reputation in the eyes of some African States. At the moment, Australia's stocks are low with most of the newly independent African countries; and this is no doubt due to our support for the present South African regime and ex-Prime Minister Menzies' bland acceptance of the position of the Smith Government in Rhodesia.

For our own advantage, quite apart from any relief that Biafra may receive, it would seem practical for the Australian Government at least to condemn Nigeria's behaviour, if not lead and fight in the United Nations for action to save the Biafrans.

Personal opinion. It would be wrong of me to suggest that there was an easy way of fixing the starvation and slaughter that was going on in Biafra. But I should point out that the above Letters, and similar sentiments from around the world, did nothing to ease the plight of the Biafrans.

Here, I am not being critical of all the well-meaning persons who were doing everything they could. It was just that no one, anywhere, could **rescue** the interested parties from situations that they had created, and which perhaps they regretted now with all of their might.

But, hold our horses. Take a deep breath. I could at this stage continue on and write about all of the afflicted countries above, just as I did for Biafra. But fortunately for all of us, space does not permit.

So I will now give you just a few Letters that point out that the other regions above have their own problems, and their own Mickey Mouse solutions.

A Letter on Russia and Czechoslovakia.

Letters, James Duncan. Between September and December, nine Russian cargo ships will arrive in Australia. Also, "it is believed that Government-owned ships of the USSR and Poland are to be sent to Australia to offer a service for cargo" and that "it is understood the USSR sailings will be two a month, and Polish sailings one a month."

Prime Minister Gorton recently censured the Soviet Union for its "gross act of perfidy (in Czechoslovakia) that should be condemned by the world" and his motion of censure was passed by the House of Representatives, 96-nil.

Surely, then, if the Federal Government is sincere in its condemnation of Russia's action in invading Czechoslovakia, it will not permit these Russian ships to carry trade from Australian ports, but will place an immediate embargo on Russian and other satellite shipping entering Australian ports.

The Government's censure motion did no harm to the Russians, and was of no real help to the Czechs. A curtailment of trade with Russia, however, is one way in which we can really help the Czech people.

Letters on Rhodesia

Letters, Fay Coutts. Mr Smith, PM of Rhodesia, is in a difficult position. He and his countrymen have taken that nation from barbarism and turned it into a civilised country, that can take its place with pride in any circumstances. They have built the nation's real assets and also the natives. They have raised all the population of the nation from poverty, disease and ignorance even to the stage where some of them can now enter the middle class.

Now the British PM Wilson wants him to hand power and assets back to the blacks. Smith says he will do this in 12 years, and **Wilson wants it now**.

Wilson should stop playing petty politics, stop bowing to all the do-gooders and seeking cheap votes, and do what is right and fair for the nation and its white population. **He should wait.**

Letters, G Secansky. The vagaries of international politics and law never fail to amaze me! It would appear that a principle which applies in one case is not applicable in another, particularly if one country is large and the other is small.

Trade sanctions have been applied against Rhodesia, and the right to participate in the Olympic Games to be held shortly in Mexico has been denied to South Africa.

On the other hand the people of Biafra have been subjected to the most horrible atrocities at the hands of the Nigerian Government, and a small country, Czechoslovakia, has been occupied by a foreign power.

How is it possible that trade sanctions and the withdrawal of the right to take part in the Olympic Games can be used to intimidate some nations, while actual violence is tolerated for reasons not disclosed?

A Letter on Sports and Politics

Letters, F Macdonald. No wonder the Olympic torch blew up and went out on its way to Mexico City. With the coincidental announcement of the Australian Government's ban on Rhodesian golfers and cricketers we must have seen everything in the way of political pressure through sport.

It beats the on-again, off-again invitation to South Africa to participate in the Olympics and the threatened boycott of the Games by the Black Power movement in the United States.

Australians are now in the happy position of being permitted to play games with Russians or Poles or East Germans, who are very busily interfering with other people at the present time; but are not allowed to play with Rhodesians who are not interfering with anyone - except Mr Harold Wilson and his amour-propre.

Is this international diplomacy? Or two-faced? Or fantastic? Or what?

A Letter criticising the world

Letters, Paul White, Transvaal. My, my, what a moral, sanctimonious bunch you Aussies and Kiwis turned out to be.

With little, if any, knowledge of what goes on here on the southern tip of Africa, you blandly denounce your friends, sever the ties created on the battlefields of the world and on our sportsfields and actively support boycotts and embargoes against us.

I presume that while this holier-than-thou attitude is upon you, you will take similar steps against say, the Russians for their rape of Czechoslovakia; or Nigeria for her genocidal war against the Biafrans; or against any of the Arab nations for their policies and aggression towards Israel; or East Germany for the Berlin Wall;

or the Congolese for the attempted genocide of the
Watutsi tribe; or China for her invasion of Mongolia;
or Kenya for legislation against her Asian population;
or Zambia for her policy of Africanisation (or don't you
know about this?).

You may have noted that in the above I haven't even
mentioned Canada, America, Australia or New Zealand
and their respective **racial attitudes past or present.**

Comment. In my 17 years of writing these books covering
30 years, I can remember **one** period that stands out as
being **a period of utmost turmoil in the world.** That,of
course was World War II.

After that, this period in 1968 runs a good second. It is
a different type of turmoil, without the **extreme** violence of
the War years. It is turmoil springing from a universal wish
for national groups to be free from foreign domination,
fired up by the prospect **that such a state might now in
fact be possible.** In Vietnam, Czechoslovakia, Rhodesia,
South Africa, in Biafra, in the USA, and dozens of other
nations, there were independence movements doing battle
long-term, one way or another, to break with the dominance
of the past.

At this time, though, there were so many of them confronting
the world daily, and none of them had as yet any hope of
solution. In the long run, as I look back, some of them have
gone away, while others remain. A few happy endings, but
in fact, for some, no ending is yet in sight.

**What a world we live in. It would be funny if it wasn't
so tragic.**

FOOTBALL FEUDS

Letters, Kerwin Maegraith. In spite of thunderous and sustained publicity in the Press, radio and TV, a mere 44,000 people, in a city of two million, turned up to watch our Rugby League semi-final, South Sydney v St George, at the Sydney Cricket Ground on Saturday! By contrast, and as usual, 106,000 screaming fans were at the Melbourne Cricket Ground to see Geelong overwhelm St Kilda in the game that is truly King in Australia, Australian Rules.

You don't have to go far to discover the reason why **Australian Rules supersedes all other games as our national attraction. It is by far the most spectacular game.** The ball travels three times the distance. The ground is larger and no other footballers can kick and handle a football like those Aussie Rules stars.

Is it any wonder then that our Rugby League cannot even get a kick in four Australian States? In Sydney Rugby League is the game, even Soccer being pushed to the sidelines. Our own code, which is the religion of four-fifths of Australian football interest, is the most spectacular of the lot. Even the most one-eyed local must realise that you can't draw 106,000 delighted fans to a football match unless you have the attraction.

Comment. It came as no surprise that there were a few replies to this Letter. As one writer said, "I need to cut these **tall-pansies** lovers down to size."

Letters, Nugget Crompton. I was wrong. I had heard that it was hard to get a Letter published in the *SMH.* But Maegraith's Letter proves it is not. Even the most idiotic Letter since the Epistles got published, so I am sure that my erudition will get through.

Let me tell you some facts. **Aerial ping-pong** will fade out in a few years, as Sydney expands, and the hicks in Melbourne benefit from the missionaries sent to save them. **Soccer** will dry up as the fans kill each other and their home countries in Europe refuse to take their bodies because they have no brains.

Rugby Union will become a sporting enclave, breeding only in GPS schools, with their fans dying of boredom waiting for a single player to do a single tackle.

In the meantime, **Rugby League** will get stronger and will consume Australia, and spread to the entire world. I can see it as being the only sport played at the 2000 Olympics.

Comment. Nugget got a few things right and a few things wrong. Melbourne now (in 2018) still sees a crowd of 100,000 at the **Aussie Rules** Grand Final. It now has National League Clubs in Sydney, Brisbane and Perth.

Soccer has lost its image as being the game of wogs and crowd violence and has grown everywhere as a game less violent than League.

Rugby League has indeed done well, and can now boast successful World Cup events, and National Clubs up and down the east coast of Australia. It also has a Club of champions in Melbourne.

Rugby Union fans are still waiting for that tackle. But alas, I fear, they will not see it from an Australian team. This sentence is printed deliberately in small print in the hope that Union fans will overlook it.

DON'T HOLD YOUR BREATH

The NSW Government said that the Sydney Opera House would be finished by 1972 and the total cost would be $85 million. When work started in 1960, the completion date was to be 1964, and the cost $5 million.

OCTOBER NEWS ITEMS

NSW teachers in State schools are officially on strike today, a Tuesday. It is expected that most teachers will participate, though many of them are against it....

The strike had been a long time coming. The teachers, of course, want more pay and better conditions. Who doesn't. But they also point to the large numbers of children in classrooms, the procrastination in creating teachers colleges, and teachers being forced to teach High School classes they are not qualified to teach....

Some of these problems have been caused by **the drain of teachers to Canada**, which is offering them better deals. This is a sore point with the Department which **pays for the training of teachers, then their blooding for a few years, only to have them poached....**

Teachers in other States have identical problems.

The Olympics Committee is getting nervous. With **only nine days** to the start of events **in Mexico City**, **a riot broke out** killing 10 people and 75 were wounded in a gun battle than lasted 90 minutes.

The Lawn Tennis Association will **receive $100,000 for TV rights** if the US makes **the Davis Cup final** in Australia in December....

This is peanuts compared to the sums paid 50 years later, but **at the time it was a staggering amount**. **$100,000 just to shoot a few sets of tennis!**

Well, what about the tennis court that sold in the Sydney suburb of Woolahra for $73,000? In 1968, that's a bit rich, The basic wage for adults is about $2,000 a year.

Stephen Leslie Bradley died yesterday in Goulbourn gaol. He was imprisoned in 1961 for the kidnapping and murder of Bondi schoolboy Graeme Thorne. **The lad was a target because his father had won a large sum in the State Lottery. He was captured and held for ransom.**

The Olympic flame arrived in Mexico. But with a difference. The ship carrying the flame anchored half a mile off Vera Cruz, and the final stage of its journey was finished off by swimmers in relay keeping the flame out of the water.

In London, 150 hippies sat outside St Pancras Station at midnight and **prayed and chanted that the Station would be moved to another site** on the other side of the Thames. Lots of violins, flutes and bells were there....

The Station did not respond. A long-haired git leading the congregation explained that this was because **two drunks**, who were laughing and abusing the chanters, **"frightened the spirits away."**

Birth of a new religion. The world headquarters of the Church of **Scientology** granted a loan of $2.6 million, interest-free, to help set up the quasi-religion in Victoria, where the cult was banned at the time....

Since then the cult has gained **a substantial following**, including film stars John Travolta and Tom Cruise. However, it has never been accepted by other Churches, and has also received bad publicity for the demands it places on its followers.

CENSORSHIP

For decades, battles had raged over our censorship rules. Various public authorities had said that certain books or films were too something-or-other for the general public, and banned them. Often the adjudication bodies were Boards of the Governments, or officers from Customs or the Police Force, or magistrates or the Chief Secretary. In recent cases concerning books, it became obvious that the officials had no literary knowledge to temper their decisions, and in one case one had relied on excerpts from the Bible to support his ban.

But despite the sporadic efforts to save the nation from filth, most books and films eventually made their way to the public, and it appears as though the censorship system, while it did not achieve much, did at least set the boundaries and told interested parties that they should not go further away from the mainstream. So, at the moment, the application of our censorship laws was haphazard and inconsistent and almost capricious but, apart from being ridiculous at the individual level, they did collectively **set the limits** to what could be classed as indecent.

There were, however, always many people who saw that danger was not only in the domain of big-ticket items, such as books and films and live theatre, but also in the every-day world around us.

Letters, R Dorman. An "oldie" protests, for a change! The vociferous group of undisciplined, "enlightened" people, in common with advertising moguls, authors, playwrights, publishers etc. are willing to allow large doses of distorted sex to wreak its insidious havoc on the minds of immature people of all ages. It seems that all that is needed today to make a "hit" of some "work of art" is to **make it more or less pornographic, labelling it "adult" or "frank."**

Let's not be mistaken - our rising rate of pack rapes, promiscuity, sex crimes and unwed mothers can be attributed to our undisciplined, permissive indulgence. If something isn't done soon to curb the influence of distorted sex, sensationalism and violence on our society, we can expect an even greater harvest of violence and depravity.

Now the authorities offer only token interference. For example, look at **the classifications put on movies and TV shows.** Perhaps some people do heed them, but I have never met any of them. At the moment, in 2018, some adult magazines are wrapped in plastic, but very few news-agents would lose a sale by raising questions about the age of a customer.

Dave Probert, Letters. The vast mass of material that might offend is left uncensored. Even if the authorities, or if the average person did want to control this, what a problem they would face. For example, a young man might be turned on by something that would leave an older man yawning. Or a grannie might be offended at any discussion of prostitutes, but a young girl might like to know the details of what the girls feel.

It you want to impose censors, you would have to have one censor for every person. Then as the person aged, and grew in wisdom, have a different censor wise enough to accommodate the ever-changing situation.

The well-meaning oldies who suggest some sort of control over everyday living should relax, perhaps read a dirty book, and leave the youth to muddle through the world as they seem to have done for quite a while.

CENSORSHIP IN WAR

Censorship in Australia towards the end of WWII was severe. Not the type of censorship we were just talking about, but rather control of information that was connected to the War activities.

For the individual at home, this meant that letters they sent to their servicemen were opened and read, and any information that was deemed to be helpful to the enemy was deleted. Letters **from** the servicemen were also opened, and information on where the soldier was, on how he was living, or where action might be, was cut out.

The message to the nation was that *Loose Lips Cost Lives*. So secret agents were constantly listening to private conversations and eagerly reporting any loose tongues. For example, a woman on a tram crossing Sydney Harbour Bridge told a neighbour that some American ships were in port. She was prosecuted, even though she, or anyone in Sydney city, could have looked out the window and seen the US naval vessels swarming with visitors.

The censorship system for individuals back home was oppressive to the ordinary citizen, and it was dubious in its results.

But there was another side to censorship that was not so obvious. **This involved the suppression of news of the War** so that the only news the people got was that permitted by the Army for dissemination.

To put it bluntly, victories were reported, or imagined, so that at all times we felt that we were winning the war, and that the enemy, cowards and inhuman, were on the run. We were the goodies, and the enemy was universally bad, we were told. If in a battle we lost 10 men, the villains lost at least 100. The Japs, we were told, were ineffective midgets, could hardly talk, were vicious, and would collapse in a heap if they would only come out of the jungle and fight like real men. This propaganda aimed to keep our citizen morale high, and production higher.

CENSORSHIP ON VIETNAM

Our authorities now announced that they intended to increase the level of wartime censorship on Vietnam.

This meant that news from Vietnam would have to pass through the Army, and we would get goody-goody accounts as in WWII.

It meant that the unwarranted shooting of an enemy by a General, as we saw in March, would not be known to the public, and that the Army would not have to face public outrage. It meant, at a time when the US forces were causing more and more "collateral damage", we innocents at home would be spared the knowledge of the consequences.

Many individuals and Press-related organisations protested. This long letter below represents well the chorus of views.

Letters, G Burgoyne, President, Australian Journalists' Association. These regulations, the full details of which the Defence Department refuses even to **reveal, constitute a deliberate attempt to** gag the Press. They are not motivated by a desire for greater security for the Australian troops serving in Vietnam but **by domestic political considerations**. A handful of backbench Liberal members have succeeded in convincing the Government that its interests are best served by imposing restrictive censorship regulations to ensure only Army handouts reach the Australian public as to the progress of the Vietnam war.

The new regulations are framed in such a fashion as to place impossible obstacles in the path of any journalist seeking to cover adequately the Australian end of Vietnam operations. Defence personnel in Vietnam have been prohibited from discussing with newsmen any matter which is subject to public or political controversy, and any defence or Service matter related to policy, administration, plans, conditions of service or equipment. They are prohibited from giving any impressions derived from their Service activities.

This means that, barring the gift of clairvoyance, the Australian journalist covering his own troops' activities either cables official handouts or nothing at all.

During the three years that Australian troops have been serving in Vietnam there has not been a single breach of security. At no time have Australian troops been endangered by journalistic coverage. **To pretend that the new regulations are introduced as a security measure is impossible.** To allow the regulations to be imposed without objection would be to agree to a fundamental curtailment of freedom.

This committee has protested to the Prime Minister, Mr Gorton, the Minister for Defence, Mr Fairhall, and the Minister for the Army, Mr Lynch. We cannot be silent. We hope that others feel sufficiently strongly about their freedom to protest also. Mr Gorton should remember his remarks at the Australian Journalists' Association summer school for professional journalism on February 2 this year: "I believe that Governments ought never to seek to suppress news or information, whether those Governments feel it is for the moment to their advantage to do it or not to their advantage to do it."

If there is anything more to say, the Letter below does that.

Letters, Gordon Jenkins. The worst point about the Army's Vietnam censorship rules is the implication that the Armed Services consider journalists untrustworthy.

In World War II when I was responsible for "public relations" and censorship for the Indian Armed Forces and subsequently in similar posts for the British Commonwealth Forces in Singapore, Malaya and Japan (after the war) the policy was to give journalists every possible assistance to do their job, including freedom of movement and talk among the troops, and as much off-the-record information as could be revealed.

It was the journalists' job to inform the world outside our area, and it was my job to help them. Yet I cannot recall one instance of a journalist failing to honour this trust or of knowingly being responsible for any so-called "security breach."

Comment. When a Government makes up its mind, it is very hard to change it. Despite the Press and other powerful forces being against it, the new regulations were enforced.

But, as you will find out when I do my last piece on Vietnam, in December, the embargoes broke down when the atrocities blamed on the Americans were revealed later in the war.

PROSTITUTES IN THE NEWS AGAIN

Every Australian government, State or Federal, every now and then, gets a rush of blood to the head and talks about getting tough on crime. Right now, the NSW authorities decided that Police should be given **the power to enter brothels** and collect the girls and customers and pimps, and charge them with any of several offences.

This stirred up discussion of the future that some people would like to see for the industry.

Letters, (Dr) G Charles. The prostitution rackets will simply be driven into other, more devious channels; the gangsters will still have their control; bribery and corruption will be intensified; and the police will be given even greater powers to attack the civil liberties of individuals who, for various reasons, may have incurred their displeasure.

Why is it that politicians resolutely refuse to face the facts of life? Year after year the Commonwealth is importing tens of thousands of virile single men, who want, and expect to have, regular sexual intercourse. They have almost no chance of obtaining it in the way that most of the indigenous male population do, that is through normal social contacts.

Licensed brothels, properly controlled, would, at one stroke, supply the need, and cut out almost all the racketeering that is inevitable with either the present system or the Chief Secretary's proposed legislation. They might even do something to reduce the alarming increase in rape, and by regular medical inspections help to reduce the rapidly rising incidence of venereal disease.

Letters, R Caldwell. Dr Charles has made some telling points in his advocacy of licensed brothels, but he is wrong in blaming politicians for "refusing to face the facts of life." Politicians, after all, are the mirror of those who put them there and cannot be expected to launch forth boldly into a major and controversial revolution. A politician who said "I am going to establish licensed brothels" would be denounced from almost every pulpit and public association in the land; one can hardly imagine any women's organisation praising his far-sightedness.

Letters, Estella Camhi. In the best interests of society, the services of a prostitute should be made available as **a medical benefit under the NHS.** There are countless individuals whose physical and emotional health is undermined by the lack of a suitable partner. These unfortunate individuals often have to resort to anti-social, destructive outlets in an effort to cope.

Physiotherapy is allowed; why not sexual therapy? A physician or psychiatrist should be allowed to refer a patient to a prostitute (perhaps a more salubrious title might be "libidologist") if he feels such therapy is warranted for the patient's well-being. The cost to the community would be far less than the amount now spent on tranquillisers, barbiturates, excessive use of other drugs and alcohol. It would just be a matter of transferring beds from mental institutions to other sites.

When are people going to wake up to the fact that the reason it has been impossible to eradicate prostitution is that it is an essential service to a significant section of the population?

Letters, Nita Schultz. Is Miss Estella Camhi serious in recommending prescribed sexual promiscuity as therapy for disordered masculine nerves? Is this the result of all this half-baked humanism that is being substituted for an adult philosophy nowadays?

If the sex game can be said to have been proved a social necessity because it has survived, the same might be said of alcohol, drugs, crime and even modern products such as detergents, all of them over-advertised.

The problem of masculine frustration is not properly the concern of women, excepting perhaps sentimental spinsters and prostitutes themselves. The normal sexual relationship between man and woman is marriage, and if young male migrants insist on travelling while knowing in advance of the deprivations they may be called upon to bear, that is their own problem.

Letters, W Jennings. Prostitutes are human beings with human feelings, despite society's disdainful view of them. They are not mere carnal devices to allay male libidos. Every effort should be made **to rehabilitate them**, not to legalise their activities.

If Australia has an excess of unmarried males let us encourage **a greater female immigration** and not introduce a degrading expedient.

The State Government is to be commended for its new vice legislation. In this matter it is pleasing that **the Government apparently seeks eradication rather than exploitation of a serious social problem**.

Letters, St Thomas. A number of writers rather furtively said that humans are born with a sexual need built in to them. There is virtually nothing they can do about it. Some religious people say they can suppress the sex drive, but no one can suggest that leads to a satisfactory life. But there are many, many people who are plain ugly or unattractive because of some feature or aspect of personality. **They cannot attract partners.**

Society does not provide for these. What are they supposed to do? Their sex drives are built in, but they can scarcely and intermittently control them, and there is no one to express their feelings with.

They find their own solutions. One way is to visit prostitutes. But **whatever they do, there seems to be no way that will satisfy society**. Enough of this rubbish about cold showers and offering the pain up to God for supposed sins.

Society, it's time to start talking.

1968 TV SHOWS:

Bandstand

Homicide

Skippy the Bush Kangaroo

This Day Tonight

Bob Dyer's Pick-A-Box

Star Trek

Days of Our Lives

Doctor Who

The Saint

I Dream of Jeannie

1968 RADIO PROGRAMS:

Blue Hills

Argonauts' Club (ABC Children's Hour)

John Laws and Race Results

Sentimental Journey

Hit Parade of Classics with John Dease

My Word and My Music

Readings from the Bible

Andrea

The Country Hour
Cricket

NOVEMBER NEWS ITEMS

Authorities in Australia are **conducting tests on the levels of tar in cigarettes** sold in Australia. They are becoming receptive to the idea that smoking **may** cause cancer, and are toying with the idea of **labelling packets of cigarettes with their tar content**....

That is as far as it yet goes. There is no suggestion so far of any campaign that directly links smoking and cancer.

Sir William Yeo, President of the NSW **RSL**, was talking at a National Congress about **the oath of allegiance that members were forced to swear**. It contained a reference to the other Members of the British Commonwealth.....

He objected to this because **that Commonwealth was now "a polyglot lot of wogs, bogs, logs and dogs...."**

He refused to apologise. In fact he added that the African member nations were "strike me pink, **all bloody butchers**. The majority of them have not achieved anything in the democratic way of government. The Nigerians are butchering their own people in Nigeria, and other African nations were leaning toward Communism, as was India...."

His remarks caused much embarrassment and smoothing out in diplomatic and government circles.

The Melbourne Cup will interrupt the nation's business again next Tuesday....

A punter from Mackay, on the north Queensland coast, **has booked a taxi for the 1,700 mile trip**, and return, to Melbourne....

The trip is currently under way. It will cost the punter $480. **This will cover the cost of the taxi, and accommodation for the punter and driver for a week.**

Dick van Dyke was an American comedian, who was a rarity among his breed because he was actually funny. His brother was also a comedian, and was doing a tour of Australia. He was to be joined by his wife and daughter in a few days....

On arrival, the daughter was refused entry, because she had not been given a smallpox injection. She was given the choice **of staying in a quarantine station for two weeks, or flying out immediately.** She chose the latter. She was allowed **10 minutes** with her father before leaving.

What happened to all the jokers? During WWII and for 20 years after, any group of 10 people could always produce **one person who had an endless string of jokes** that could be told flawlessly. Some of them dirty, but most of them not. Shaggy dog stories, Pat and Mick stories, and Englishmen, Irishman and Scotsmen stories. Plus lots of freelance stories.....

Where have such people gone?

Rain Lover **won The Cup.** Over in the USA, **the other race was won by Richard Nixon,** a Republican. Nixon won the most College of Electors votes, but was about square in terms of the popular vote....

Nixon had vowed that **his first move would be to end the Vietnam War.** He was probably sincere in this, **but he did not achieve his promise.**

AMERICAN PLAY BOYS

The young lads from America, who were fighting in the Vietnam war, were deciding in increasing numbers that they wanted to come to Australia for their **Rest and Recreation** leave.

There was a popular image of them that they swanned into this nation, and that wine, women, and fighting the locals in pubs was their sole interest. There were many people here who were saying that they should not come, and despite the mass of American dollars they brought with them, we would be better off without them.

But there was another side to their visits, one that did not get much play in the press.

Letters, Doris Cheesbrough. I am making a plea for more young American Servicemen here on R and R leave to be welcomed into Australian homes.

Since placing my name at the R and R centre, I have been besieged with requests to have them in our home. This I have done to the best of my ability, in a natural no-fuss style, which seems to have been appreciated. Spread over a short time, two have come to stay with us for their entire leave (six days), and on five other occasions we have had one or two for afternoon and evening visits, including car trips and a hearty meal. In every case we have found them courteous, interesting, easy to entertain and most grateful.

Comment. This was not just an isolated experience. It was common. These were just young boys, ripped out of their families, just as our boys were. Many of them wanted their Mom and Apple Pies, just as **our** boys wanted their Australian equivalents.

WOGS AND BOGS

Sir William Yeo was elected as President of the NSW Branch of the Returned Servicemens League in 1949. This was a supposedly non-political position, but Yeo took many public stances that placed him fully in the political mainstream. He was a fierce anti-Communist, a staunch defender of the White Australia Policy, a stern critic of Japan, and a strong campaigner for greater war effort in Korea, Malaya, and Vietnam.

His latest outburst against members of the British Commonwealth was consistent with many of his previous utterances, and by now his influence was being diminished by the embarassment that he often caused for the RSL.

In late October, he was getting into hot water. He persuaded the National Executive to amend its Constitution so that it could suspend or expel any Member whose conduct "is subversive to League policies." When interpreted into Yeo-speak, this meant that **any person who spoke anywhere against the Vietnam war would be expelled**. Soon after this, he advocated that **any student protestor charged by a Cour**t for offensive behavior in an anti-war demonstration **should be expelled from university**.

Many rank-and-file Members of the League were outraged. While all this was being fomented, he made his comments about the *wogs* in the British Commonwealth, and his position grew more precarious.

The *SMH* was first cab off the rank. The Editor said, of Sir William, that even when he is most boorish and intolerant, one is tempted to take his remarks as those of a harmless old fogey. But, he went on, in the case of calling people *wogs*, **he is not being harmless**. He speaks as a Knight of the Realm, and as the representative of the ex-Servicemen of the nation. If the League wants to maintain is position as a responsible force in community affairs, **its only option was to accept Sir William's resignation**. Other writers had their say.

Letters, Peter D Kelly. As some of his friends at the time may recall, RSL State President Sir William Yeo remarked shortly after his election 20 years ago...

"Before I get too old, decrepit and a bloody fool, I hope someone has the good sense to knock me over the skull with a bit of four-by-two"... or words to that effect.

Since his latest boorish outburst has embarrassed every second member of the RSL - indeed, every second Australian - and despite two decades of unmatched and magnificent service to ex-Servicemen, it's surely time that someone granted old Bill his wish.

Letters, David Dale. Recent motions passed at the RSL conference have convinced me that the RSL is moving more and more towards the very philosophy which its members fought against in World War II. Led by a number of intolerant reactionaries, the RSL now appears to condone militarism, nationalism and suppression of dissent.

For example, it is now RSL policy that any university student convicted of demonstrating violently against the present Government should be expelled from university. Surely the law provides sufficient punishment for those who break it.

Letters, (Dr) Keith Cochrane. It took our company nearly 20 years to build up goodwill with businessmen from the Far East, which is only several hours away by plane.

Sir William Yeo, in a matter of minutes, has inflicted irreparable damage to our nation by an unprovoked open insult to delegates representing our friends in Africa and Asia, calling them "wogs and bogs, etc."

It now becomes imperative for all ex-Servicemen to unite and call for Sir William Yeo's resignation.

Letters, E Walker. The suggestion by T Mitchell, MLA, that a posthumous knighthood should be bestowed upon Captain Cook has little to commend it to the Australian public.

As Captain James Cook, RN, the famous navigator has a memory known and revered throughout the world. As **Sir** James Cook, he could be elevated to the stature of a **Sir** William Yeo.

A minority thought Bill was pretty good.

Letters, J Sutherland. How refreshing to read old Bill Yeo's plain speaking in the "Herald." After all the mealy-mouthed humbug that goes on in high places about the so-called "British Commonwealth", it's great to find a man in public life with the honesty and courage to say what he really thinks.

Letters, Robert Forsyth. I was greatly heartened by the recent RSL motion urging the expulsion of any university student convicted of taking part in a demonstration against our Government's foreign policy. My only criticism is that this move would still be too lenient.

Comment. The few people who supported Sir William were not enough to save him. He protested into the next year and then resigned.

COLOUR TV

TV had come to Australia in 1956. This was about 20 years after Britain and the USA. We got it just in time for the 1956 Olympic Games. Likewise, we were well behind in switching to colour.

With the original black-and-white transmission, our society had struggled with questions about whether we should have just a single broadcaster like the BBC in England at the time. Or whether we should have lots of commercial stations, as in the USA.

There were other questions such as what hours should broadcasts be restricted to, and how religion should be pumped onto the air waves. We wended our way through successfully, and now came the question of adding colour.

Of course, apart from the costs of transmission, this meant that TV sets across the nation would have to be replaced. The biggest question we thus had, this time, was whether that cost was worth it.

Letters, R Dorman. Surely the Commonwealth Government is not giving serious consideration to the introduction of colour television?

How can this unnecessary and expensive luxury be justified when our education system is in such dire need of financial assistance, not to mention our hospitals, roads and many other more important and productive services?

If we have such a surplus of money here that we have to waste it on pretty pretty TV, surely we could give some to our aged people, pensioners, etc., or even to suffering humanity overseas.

Letters, Hilary Cronin. New colour TV sets will require more complicated technology. We will find, if we switch to them, that they will be so complex, that our manufacturers will not be able to make them or service them.

We will end up losing our own local industries to American giants.

Letters, Peter Pritchard. Have we got the tiger by the tail? If we go to colour TV, will we go to bigger screens soon in the future? Then perhaps to better sound, and or perhaps to a better grade of image?

Could the sets become major items of furniture, and have radios in them? What about multiple sets in the one house?

Marketing is grabbing hold of this nation and the world. We all think that what we have now is the best, the very best. But that is just what **we** think. Our marketing gurus think differently.

My bet is that we will be gradually shamed into buying one upgrade after another of TV sets, and every one of them will be more expensive than the others.

My solution is to say *no* to colour and stick to our perfectly good black-and-white.

Comment. I rarely intervene but I must say that this is one of the silliest Letters I have ever seen. What a lot of tripe. This will never happen.

MORE ON SCIENTOLOGY

By now, the **almost hysterical opposition** to Scientology in some quarters had resulted in South Australia and Victoria banning the cult. Western Australia is considering similar legislation. NSW had looked at similar bans, but **decided against any actions against the religion**.

It was argued that they were wrong in doing so. After all, a Royal Commission in Victoria and a public enquiry in Britain had found ample evidence that the teachings and pressures and recruiting techniques of the cult can have pernicious effects on some mentally weak or sick people.

Against this was the fact that Scientology put itself forward as a religion. It practices and beliefs might be seen by some as in the realms of crackpots, but that could be said by outsiders of most religions.

On top of that, the *SMH* said, there is adequate protection at law against intimidation, fraud, false pretences, assault and intimidation, and the other practices that Scientologists are often accused of, and there is no need for special legislation to bolster those laws.

As the *Herald* said, "it is to the Government's credit that it **resisted** the unhealthy clamour for a ban on Scientology as if the tuppeny-halfpenny cult, with its mumbo-jumbo and absurd theories, were the cause of all our social evils."

The general population agreed, at least as seen in the Sydney Press.

Letters, Rosemary Howe. Congrats on the leading article on scientology and the banning of cults.

It is appalling to ban any belief or idea which does not appeal to society as a whole. The inherent dangers in such movements as scientology are obvious, but once a law is passed it can take hundreds of years to repeal it.

With the growing improvement in education generally, intelligence alone will be enough to "ban" subversive and distorted cults and beliefs through mature insight into what such cult or belief has to offer.

No one who is capable of analytical or mature thought could possibly fall for the blandishments of any religion not thoroughly based on the positive ideal of the brotherhood of man, and this is the only safeguard society ever needs.

Personal Comment. The Church of Scientology, both here and overseas, has continued to grow, and also to pick up some celebrities. At the same times, other non-conventional churches have thrived, none more so than the Hillsong Pentacostal Church in Australia.

This emphasises that the general population is finding less value in theology and a detailed study of religion and its history, and is seeing Church-going and good works as their focus. As one good Catholic said to me recently "Action and good works is replacing navel gazing."

LONDON TO SYDNEY ROAD MARATHON

After the folly of the Redex round-Australia car trials of the 1950's was recognised, there was not much interest in repeating them. That is, **until this race from London to Sydney was proposed**. Then the support became vocal, but so too did the opposition.

Letters, A Parkinson. Could you tell me how official approval was obtained for the 1968 London-Sydney road marathon to be run on our public roads.?

This "marathon" is in every sense of the word a "race," and in all States it is a police offence to conduct anything in the nature of a "race" on public roads. As widely publicised, it is a "car-breaking, man-breaking race," which will indeed break most of the cars and their crews, and perhaps a few innocent road-users.

Following the maniacal behaviour of drivers in a number of Australian road reliability trials some years ago - which, incidentally, left all the State branches of the Australian Road Safety Council quite unconcerned - the Australian Road Safety Council itself unanimously condemned the holding of further trials on public roads.

But a patron of the Australian Road Safety Council, no less than the Prime Minister, Mr Gorton, himself, has just given his blessing to this international demonstration of crazy driving against the clock, day and night, without sufficient rest and sleep, and much of the time on dangerous roads and under bad weather conditions. **This** has now the highest official approval!

If driving illegally thus in road marathons is approved by the Prime Minister and the police authorities, it must certainly encourage many other drivers, particularly the younger ones, to organise their own little "marathons" whenever they feel so inclined.

The rev-heads won, and the race went ahead. Amid much excitement, the race started from London with 100 cars and sped across Europe to Bombay. 73 survived and went to sea. They landed in Perth, and then raced to Melbourne and Sydney following normal rules for such marathons.

En route, there were some interesting touches. For example, the Australian police were not at all pleased to see them. On arrival in Perth, all vehicles were inspected to see that they were roadworthy by Australian standards. Defects had to be fixed. Also, they were booked during the journey for all breaches of traffic rules.

Another tit-bit was that as the leader neared Nowra, 98 miles from Sydney, he hit a Mini Minor head-on and the race car and driver were both wrecked. This was on a section of the road that was supposedly closed to the public. The Mini Minor was being driven by a pair of off-duty policemen who, it was rumoured, were "as drunks as skunks."

The Marathon was a huge success, and there were follow-ups in 1993, 2000 and 2003. The Australian team came third. Sir Frank Packer, of Sydney's *Daily Telegraph,* was a sponsor for the Australian leg.

LIVE THEATRE IN SYDNEY

Charley's Aunt

Fiddler on the Roof

The Boys in the Band

Oh What a Lovely War

Merry Wives of Windsor

Mother Goose

The Prime of Miss Jean Brodie

Man of La Mancha

Googie Withers and John McCallum

The Crucible

King Lear

America Hurrah

The Wayne Newton Show

Barry Humphries

Notes: Googie Withers and John McCallum were a husband and wife team.

Wayne Newton was, on arrival, almost unheard of in Australia. He was a big success here and, of course, **big** as well.

Barry Humphries introduced Edna Everage as a character in 1955. She became a Dame in 1972.

Mother Goose and King Lear were **not** here in person. It was the shows with their names that were here.

DECEMBER NEWS ITEMS

Breath testing of motorists in NSW will be introduced in **mid-December**. It will not be random, being used only when there are signs of intoxication or traffic offences. The .08 per cent blood alcohol level will apply.....

Kits for do-it-yourself testing are selling out in chemists' shops. The kits have visible crystals in them that turn green if the legal limit is exceeded. They are for single-only use, and are quite cheap....

There is a big run on them at the moment as **wives buy them**, supposedly for the **use of their husbands over the Christmas period.**

A seven-year-old boy was killed when **he was sucked into a wheat bin** near the NSW town of Barellan. His father and grandfather were nearby but did not know he was in the bin until it was nearly empty.

Stockmen of the Gurindji tribe in the Northern Territory will go back to work after **a strike that started three years ago.** They walked off the job because of disputes over wages, and as a **demand for the return of tribal lands....**

They are returning to work now because **the new pay rates, set by law**, will apply. This will **give them parity with white workers. The land dispute continues on.**

A family of six in Britain sold their home and car, and dug into their savings. They bought a 30-foot catamaran, and **set sail for Australia**, via the West Indies....

The youngest child is aged three months. The family were driven out of England by the high cost of living.

A blow-out at the drilling platform has allowed huge streams of gas to escape from BHP's drilling platform in Bass Strait. **The gas is not ablaze**, but is bubbling furiously upwards and **weakening the 16 legs on the platform which will collapse**....

The only hope to save the well and the platform is to force mountains of cement down the well and plug it.....

The **famous Red Adair** hopefully will come in and save the day. **BHP shares took a big dive on the news.**

The Title Fight, between World Champion Australian Bantamweight Lionel Rose and his Mexican challenger, definitely **will be broadcast by radio** from America....

And it **might** be telecast as well. It all depends on the American Space Agency, **NASA**. It has **first rights to the satellite**, and it might need it at the time of the fight.

Rose won the fight but the **pro-Mexican crowd ripped the stadium to shreds** after the points decision....

Rose was shocked by the riot. He said "Those bloody Mexicans. See the cuts to my manager, and his bleeding. **They were animals. They can stick their fights.**"

NSW held local elections, without compulsion. The turn-out was only 35 per cent. The immediate question was whether **to return to compulsory voting**.

Red Adair said that fixing the platform blow-out would take **two more weeks,** and might not end in saving it.

A twelve-sided 50 cent coin will be introduced soon.

John Gorton was proving to be a restful Prime Minister with **an agenda for change that was not over-full**. When asked what he would be doing during the Christmas break, he replied "what I hope to do is **get on a ship in Fiji** and spend a week coming back to Australia - **having a bludge, I suppose you would call it.** "

The Pope had his say too. "**The Church** is in an hour of unquiet, of self-criticism, one would say **even an hour of self destruction....**"

Comment. The Church did not self destruct, but since **his ruling on the Pill, there have remained many more spaces in the pews than previously.**

On December 22nd, **three American astronauts** went aboard a spaceship **called Apollo 8**, and went for a trip into space. It took them to **the "dark side" of the moon,** and around it, and **then back to Earth** to splash down in the Pacific 1,000 miles off Hawaii....

The trip took about eight days, and they got some good snaps of their holiday. **The Americans were pretty pleased about it, and said so. Often....**

Britain's Flat Earth Society was not perturbed by the **photos from the space mission**. "The images do not show all the continents, and the edges of those shown are blurred and out of perspective....

"Until they show us clear images, **we will continue fighting to prove the earth is flat.**"

Christmas last year was too noisy, and people drank and ate too much, and all those visitors got on nerves after a while. So, **the Federal Government has cancelled it this year, and is considering make the ban permanent.**

TOP HITS OF 1968:

Hey Jude	The Beatles
Sadie	Johnny Farnham
Love is Blue	Paul Mauriat
Honey	Bobby Goldsboro
The Unicorn	The Irish Rovers
Those Were the Days	Mary Hopkin
Little Arrows	Leapy Lee
Whiskey on a Sunday	The Irish Rovers
Macarthur Park	Richard Harris
Hello, Goodbye	The Beatles

TOP MOVIES OF 1968:

2001: A Space Odyssey	Keir Dullea
Funny Girl	Barbra Streisand
The Love Bug	Dean Jones
Rosemary's Baby	Mia Farrow
The Producers	Gene Wilder, Zero Mostel
Bullitt	Steve McQueen
The Lion in Winter	Peter O'Toole
Planet of the Apes	Charlton Heston
The Odd Couple	Jack Lemmon
Yellow Submarine	The Beatles
The Party	Peter Sellers
The Thomas Crown Affair	Steve McQueen

COUNTRY-TOWN BUSHFIRES

November and December were terrible months for bushfires in the Eastern States. In NSW alone, 10 people were killed and 150 houses were destroyed. **The response to this in the newspapers was enormous.** In selecting material for this book, I had over 100 *SMH* Letters to choose from. This is only the **published** Letters. The total that were written and not published, and in all newspapers, must have been huge.

To make a report on the *SMH* Letters, **I put them into three classes**. **The first class** was full of praise for the efforts of the professionals and volunteers who did so much to save the lives and property and animals and bushland from devastation. In some cases, these brave people were themselves at risk, and in a few cases, they did not survive. **The outpourings of thanks and admiration and sympathy and respect were touching to read and at the same time inspirational.**

Here is a typical Letter.

Letters, Helen Somerville. It is ironic, and a fitting comment, I suppose, on human nature, to hear, after the tragic fires, all the talk about "these gallant men" and "those wonderful firefighters" - these same men who are treated in times of non-stress with rather amused tolerance and subjected to utter snide remarks such as "playing Boy Scouts." They are gallant and wonderful - but anyone can rise to the occasion in times of disaster.

These men have what is sadly lacking in our materialistic society today, a sense of civic responsibility which prompts them to give of their spare time and energy when the need is not great and, when the real time of stress arrives, they risk losing their lives, their jobs, and everything they hold dear, with no thought of personal gain.

It is to be hoped that a lesson has been learned over the last few sad days, both on a personal and national level. Let those who live in the bushfire-prone areas and who lack the energy and initiative to join the Volunteer Fire Service at least not criticise and ridicule, and let those who are the leaders of our nation realise that volunteers can't man fires for a week at a time (with just a few hours' sleep snatched at odd times) "in case" tragedies like that at Springwood occur.

If fires are a potential danger, surely squads of RAAF or Army personnel could be based in the necessitous areas - and if this isn't possible, surely the volunteers or their employers shouldn't have to lose financially by manning these areas. The Government or councils concerned should assume this financial responsibility where it is necessary. Most firms are very understanding, but smaller firms cannot carry the paying of wages without any return, no matter how understanding they are.

As for me, these men restore my often sadly depleted faith in human nature. God bless them.

The second class concerned itself with a range of fire-fighting equipment and operational matters. There was a lack of hoses, or water, or stirrup pumps or fire engines. And a lack of co-ordination and control. There was a scarcity of information at all phases of the burn. Smouldering sites became active again.

Respondents were not so laudatory here. One writer said that "we spend so much on trivia, we as a nation need to look at the ever-recurring threat of bushfires and direct our money to equipping our fighters so that they can do the job.

But money alone will not save us. Good planning is also necessary."

But there were other thoughts.

Letters, H Tosh. Last year the Warrumbungle National Park was threatened by a bushfire. The Park trust sent a party of men to fight the fire. When they arrived, they took over full control and took action diametrically opposite, I am informed, to what the local men would have done, with the result the country men pulled out in disgust, and it's history now that the Warrumbungle Park was completely burnt out, which the locals say should not have happened. This is very wrong, the local fire officer has a better topographic picture of the situation than strangers.

Is this sort of thing happening around here?

The third class had suggestions for the future. There was a mile of these. They started with suggestions that wet towels round the face brought relief in the heat and smoke. Of course, cleaning out gutters got a mention, though some one replied that clean gutters were not much help in a 100 mph fire storm.

Others talked about the role the Army and Air Force might play. Some criticised local Councils for having regulations not allowing burn-offs whenever the time was right. Tree preservation orders in Councils came under discussion. Car manufacturers were blamed for not providing properly placed ash trays, to discourage motorists from throwing cigarettes out the window.

Fire breaks cut through forests were inadequate and not maintained properly. It was hard to get permission for fire breaks given the resistance of newly forming environmentalist groups. Burn-offs were just used as excuses for beers together on Sunday mornings.

Comment. Probably, most suggestions were sensible. But they were just little bits, here and there. **The bush-fire menace is a vastly bigger problem than this nation ever recognises.**

A PERSONAL VIEWPOINT

If the Chinese government ordered that all gum trees be removed from within a country town and from a mile radius around it, it would have no personal liberties claims against it, and **it would be done.**

If that government ordered that fire-breaks, one mile wide, be cut through our forests, never mind environmental concerns, **it would be done.**

If it set up Authorities that had the power to hit the population with sticks and then hit them again with carrots, and **would get paid only if they reduced the losses of property and lives**, they would have no screams about repressive government, **it would be done.**

We in Australia don't do things that way. We live by rules that allow people much more personal freedom than the Chinese have. We rarely think about this, but that freedom may mean that we unconsciously decide we will have more losses of life and property than we would logically choose.

It seems on first thought to be silly, but equally so would be the choice to jettison our freedoms.

I leave it to you to decide which is the better way.

THE TURKEY'S GETTING FAT

Some wastrel has been spreading the rumour that Christmas had been cancelled this year. There is no truth in this, no matter how desirable it may be. In fact, from early December the newspapers had started softening up the news, and giving us goody-goody stories that suggest the world is made of fairy floss. The shops have started the endless playing of Christmas carols, and of course, there is the wonderful array of presents to tempt the most hard-bitten Scrooge to splurge.

Let me give you an example from our city retail stores.

Perfect Gift - Splayds. "They're marvellous," was the unanimous opinion voiced by guests at our outdoors Christmas party. They were discussing Splayds, with which we had set our buffet table -- naturally! They looked so elegant and so perfect for this occasion when one-handed eating was the order of the day. Other uses are for cocktail parties, picnics, TV snacks, breakfast in bed - even normal meal-times when serving chicken or apple pie or similar. They're the ideal gift - in mirror finish, 4, 6, or 8 Splayds are respectively $6, $9, or $12; in satin finish, $7.20, $10.80, and $14.40 - from department stores and better gift shops. Covered by Australian and International Patent Office registration.

"Spritzig," Everyone? "...it's the new Rose wine from Seppelts," we exclaimed, as we held aloft the bottle to be admired. We love to be first with a surprise, and Spritzig was not only a surprise but a great success at the party. "Spritzig" is a special term for wine denoting a subtle tingle, a sense of life, with bubbles to prove it. Chill in stacks of ice, and introduce it to your set .. or give a bottle or two as Christmas gifts. It's right and very refreshing at barbecues, luncheons, picnics, dinner parties ... anywhere where good wine with a hint of colour is appreciated! Spritzig is sensibly priced, $1.40 at bottle departments and stores.

Unique Gifts! Pam arrived at the party displaying her new engagement ring - a marquise diamond, chosen from Ben Boulken's magnificent collection of diamond jewellery. Being secondhand, they can be bought at 25% discount as no sales-tax is charged. Other gifts for the discriminating include rare Georgian lorgnettes in tortoiseshell and gold; solid gold swizzle sticks, gold penknives, keychains, matchboxes, etc. Also Val St Lambert crystal; heavy silver embossed goblets; and charming "little" gifts such as silver Hildersheim spoons from $2 and handbag holders for use in restaurants.

Give a Diamond Deb! Lovely long nails, perfectly cared for, are desired by most women. So a thoughtful gift to all your friends who have troublesome nails would be the means of improving them ... so give a Diamon Deb. Professional manicurists mostly use Diamon Deb Nail Stylers, because when it comes to shaping nails, they're the best! They leave old-hat nail files and emery boards for dead. The diamond-hard surface of a Diamon Deb is made of minute diamond crystals which will not split the layers of the nail, for it is the hardest abrasive surface known ... so fingernails grow longer and stronger. Get Diamon Deb from your favourite pharmacy or department store.

Comment. I particularly like the splayds, especially, as you will remember, for one-handed eating. They are ever so in. People with two hands can use them too, though managing both at the same time takes a bit of practice.

GOODBYE TO VIETNAM

In the months prior to the US Presidential election, President Johnson lost public support rapidly. So much so that he decided not to run for re-election. The drop in his popularity was due solely to the fact that Americans were sick of a war they were not winning and the big drain on manpower and resources that it was making.

When Nixon came into office in early 1969, he instigated a slow process of withdrawal from Vietnam, which took out a fair number of troops, but left a bigger number there. Later in 1969, **US support for the war took two hits.**

Firstly, there was the My Lai massacre, in which a US Army platoon raped and killed the citizens of a village. Much near-live footage of this was relayed to the US public on TV. **Second**, was the Green Beret Affair where eight Special Forces soldiers, including a high ranking officer, were arrested for the murder of a suspected double agent. Both of these raised international and domestic outrage. On top of that, the "collateral damage" from napalm bombs continued to outrage the world.

Public support for the war plummeted, and the number of US troops was reduced a bit at a time. The US signed a peace accord signalling a full withdrawal in early 1973. The war between North and South Vietnam, however, went on, until the North over-ran the South. Peace between the two was signed in 1975.

In Australia, we watched the events in the US day by day, and the support for the war **fell** here just as it did in America. We withdrew from the war at about the same pace as our American friends, but we avoided the scandals that embroiled them.

When peace came, it was a sorry end to a bad chapter in American history. The US had entered a purely political war, with no direct threat to its well-being, and they prosecuted it for almost a decade, with huge losses. In the process, they had just about destroyed two nations, and left the North in control just it would have been if there had been no war.

I will not flog the point that this was essentially the same for Australia. We had nothing to show for it, only the rolls of the dead, and the thousands who had been wounded both visible and psychologically.

SUMMING UP 1968

Let me talk for a minute as though the Vietnam war had not happened.

Australia in 1968 did well for itself. It traded quite well overseas, and our balance of payments ended about the same as it started. The Brits continued their slow process of joining the EU, begun in 1967, at about the same pace as they are leaving it in 2018. For our part, we were learning to live without the preferential trade deals we were losing with the UK, and Asia was coming more and more into our sights.

Internally, our standard of living was high for those in work, and our safety net for the unemployed and the elderly was as good as the best anywhere. Jobs were plentiful, housing was being built or renovated at an increasing rate,

The family car could be afforded by most families, grass was being turned into lawn by the new petrol lawn mowers, Mr Whippy and his *Green Sleeves* serenaded us on Sunday afternoons, and the Hills Hoists added to the beauty of the suburban landscape. It felt like God was in the Heavens, and the sun was in the sky.

A few big events stuck out for the year. Gorton came lethargically to power, and Pope said no Pills for him. Billy Graham converted the already faithful, and Wally Mellish got great ratings on talk-back radio. Martin Luther King and Edward Kennedy were assassinated, and this gave impetus to Black Power in the US, and to independence movements elsewhere. Prostitution hit the headlines a few times, and some people were deciding whether they wanted these new home units or not. The various authorities excelled themselves by imposing censorship on civilians, and bushfires did what they do every year.

In all, then it was a pretty good year. I happen to know that the next two years will be much the same. In Tasmania, the Labor Party will lose power after 35 years, and a huge mining boom, spear-headed by Poseidon Nickel, will stir the stock markets. A couple of Americans will go for a stroll on the moon.

The following year, 185,000 migrants will arrive in Australia, Melbourne's West Gate bridge will collapse killing 35 people, and the *Indian Pacific* will make its first trip from Sydney to Perth.

None of these events will be epoch-making, and the scene could be described as business as usual.

But, back to the beginning of this Section, war in Vietnam did happen. It **did** cast a shadow over the nation in 1968, and it **will** over the next few years. The demos **will** continue, the arguments at barbies **will** continue, and our boys and men **will** continue to be killed and maimed.

For now, all we knew of the future for certain was that Richard Nixon had been elected as President. We could see that he could talk tough, and we had no idea of what this might bring. As it turned out, he also had no idea. We did know that he had been in Australia in 1953, and that he was most unpopular with the Press and others as Vice President. So, at **the end of 1968, we had not a clue of where it all was going**. Who Nixon really was, and what he might do was anyone's guess.

Thus the future in Vietnam was a mystery. If we had been told, as you have been told, that there was an end in sight, and that our troops would eventually come home, there would have been a slight sigh of relief. But no one could be told anything, and so the existing tensions just grew bigger. In particular, in the next two years, the demos got much bigger and more violent, and the nation was split further and further.

So, how can I summarise all this? I can't really. The best **one-line**r I can come up with is **"that we had a good thing going, with one outstanding problem."**

So, I ask you to accept this as a working summary. But keep in mind that "the one outstanding problem" was probably **the biggest problem that this nation faced in the second half of the 20th Century.** In all, it cost us 521 lives, over 3000 were wounded in body, and countless others were damaged in mind.

So, I will end this book, and perhaps this series of books, with the hopefully immortal words:

LEST WE FORGET

In 1949, Reds in China could rest from their Long March, and the Reds in Australia took a battering in the pits. The rabbits ruled the paddocks, and some Churches suffered from outbreaks of dirty dancing and housie. Immigration Minister Calwell crudely enforced the White Australia Policy, so that huge crowds on the beaches were nervous about getting a tan. There was plenty of petrol for motorists in NZ and Britain, but not here.

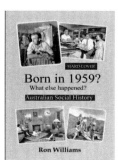

In 1959, Billy Graham called us to God. Perverts are becoming gay. The Kingsgrove Slasher was getting blanket press coverage. Tea, not coffee, was still the housewife's friend. Clergy were betting against the opening of TABs. Errol, a Tasmanian devil, died. So too did Jack Davey. There are three ways to kill a snake. Aromarama is coming to your cinema.

****

Chrissi and birthday books for Mum and Dad and Aunt and Uncle and cousins and family and friends and work and everyone else.

Don't forget a good read and chuckle for yourself.

At boombooks.biz

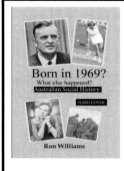

Born in 1969?
What else happened?
Australian Social History
HARD COVER
Ron Williams

In 1969, Hollywood produced a fake movie that appeared to show a few Americans walking on the moon. There are now no Labor governments in office in all Australia, but Laborites should not worry because Paul Keating just got a seat in Canberra. Thousands of people walked the streets in demos against the Vietnam War,

****